KEYSTONE IN THE ARCH

UKRAINE IN THE EMERGING SECURITY ENVIRONMENT OF CENTRAL AND EASTERN EUROPE

SHERMAN W. GARNETT

CARNEGIE ENDOWMENT FOR INTERNATIONAL PEACE

© 1997 by the
Carnegie Endowment for International Peace
2400 N Street, N.W.
Washington, D.C. 20037
Tel.(202) 862-7900
Fax.(202) 862-2610

Keystone in the Arch: Ukraine in the Emerging Security Environment of Central and Eastern Europe
may be ordered ($14.95) from Carnegie's distributor,
Brookings Institution Press,
Department 029, Washington, D.C. 20042-0029, USA.
Tel. 1-800-275-1447 or 202-797-6258.
Fax 202-797-6004.

Edited by Valeriana Kallab.
Design by Paddy McLaughlin Concepts & Design.
Printed by Automated Graphic Systems.

Library of Congress Cataloging-in-Publication Data

Garnett, Sherman W., 1955-
Keystone in the arch: Ukraine in the emerging security
environment of Central and Eastern Europe/ Sherman W. Garnett.
p. cm.
Includes bibliographical references.
ISBN 0-87003-101-5
1. Ukraine—Foreign relations—1991- 2. National security—Europe,
Central. 3. National security—Europe, Eastern. 4. World
politics, 1989- I. Title.
DK508.849.G37 1997
327.477—dc21   97-10997
                                                              CIP

To my parents,
Jacqueline and Sherman Garnett

CONTENTS

FOREWORD

Russia and the countries all-too-conveniently called "the other post-Soviet states" are a major focus of the Carnegie Endowment's work. Our Washington-based Russian-Eurasian Studies Program and our public policy center in Moscow, established in 1993, constitute a long-term institutional commitment to intellectual collaboration among scholars and specialists in the United States and the region. Our associates in Washington and Moscow—now numbering fifteen senior staff members—form complementary halves of an ambitious, comprehensive program of joint research, discussion, and publication.

Senior Associate Sherman W. Garnett, who co-chairs our project on Security and National Identity, has devoted much of his work to "the other post-Soviet states," contributing greatly to a much-needed understanding of them in their own right, not merely as derivatives of Russia's real or perceived interests. Among "the others," Ukraine is the most strategically important for its size, location, and stabilizing potential. As Garnett vividly puts it, Ukraine can be the "keystone" of a new security arch that reaches from the Baltic to the Black Sea.

This book is the first comprehensive post–Cold War study of Ukraine's critical role. Sherman Garnett sees an independent and stable Ukraine to be as crucial to the sovereignty and stability of the states of Central and Eastern Europe as a democratically evolving Russia and a strong NATO. He warns that a NATO-centric view of Ukraine's security role misses the point: the real issue is not whether Ukraine eventually becomes a member of the Alliance, but how the U.S. and other Western governments can help to ensure in the coming decade that Kiev becomes the principal stabilizer among "the other outsiders" and defines itself in relation to the expanding Alliance in a way that does not further complicate an already difficult relationship with Russia.

Dr. Garnett shows that not only Ukraine's immensity and centrality, but also its ethnic, religious, and economic diversity, will profoundly shape the geopolitics of Central and Eastern Europe. Contrary to dire Western predictions of a collapse into "suicidal nationalism," multiethnic, multiregional Ukraine has managed—even while struggling under the strains of political and economic transition and working to establish constructive relationships with its neighbors—to promote an inclusive form of democratic nationalism. That achievement is fragile—it could fall apart—but it is tremendously significant, for the viability of complex states such as Ukraine will do much to determine whether Europe and the world in the twenty-first century will be as bloody as they were in the twentieth.

Despite Ukraine's importance, Garnett points out, for most of the post–Cold War period U.S. and Western policy toward Ukraine has been fraught with misconception and neglect, excepting the concerted efforts to resolve nuclear issues. Though the bilateral agenda has broadened since 1995, Washington's engagement with Kiev remains more tactical and opportunistic than strategic and sustained. Garnett explains why this must change and how that might be accomplished.

In architecture, a keystone is defined as a part or force on which associated things depend for support—a bondstone, the wedge-shaped piece at the crown of an arch—which is inserted last and locks other pieces in place. There is, however, one major difference in practical application between architecture and policy, and it is the crux of Garnett's policy prescriptions: policymakers cannot wait until last for Ukraine to be inserted as the keystone of peace in Central and Eastern Europe.

The U.S. and other Western governments must help Ukraine perform its stabilizing function *now* by fostering its integration, especially economically, into Europe, and by encouraging the normalization of Ukrainian-Russian relations. Otherwise, the arch of security they hope to see built may never leave the drawing boards.

The views expressed and conclusions reached in this study are, of course, the author's own.

Morton I. Abramowitz, *President*
Carnegie Endowment for International Peace

March 1997

KEYSTONE IN THE ARCH

UKRAINE
IN THE NEW SECURITY ENVIRONMENT
OF CENTRAL AND EASTERN EUROPE

INTRODUCTION

I n his 1915 essay on "The Historical Evolution of the Ukrainian Problem," Mykhaylo Hrushevsky—Ukraine's greatest historian and president of the short-lived Central Rada government—predicted that "if present events do not bring about a solution," Ukraine "will remain a source of new convulsions."[1] These convulsions, Hrushevsky said, would come if the Ukrainian people were deprived of a state of their own and had to continue living as part of larger empires. The attempts of several Ukrainian governments—the Central Rada, the West Ukrainian Republic, and the Hetmanate—to establish an independent state between 1917 and 1921 could not, however, withstand internal chaos and external pressure from the German, White, and Bolshevik armies. The Ukrainian Soviet Socialist Republic (SSR) that was later created served not as a "source of new convulsions," but as one of the industrial, agricultural, and military pillars of the Soviet state. In the ultimate irony, the reunification of the Ukrainian lands was effected not by followers of Hrushevsky, but by Stalin.

Unlike Poland, which was partitioned before Europe's eyes in the eighteenth century and intruded quite forcefully on Europe's attention at key moments throughout the nineteenth and early twentieth centuries, Ukraine remained largely unknown in the West. Kiev was not on the grand tour. Most Westerners—like Russia's own historians—have viewed Ukraine as an integral part of Russia. The Hapsburgs, the Romanovs, and other neighbors had to contend with Ukrainian national aspirations, but Western Europe was never pressed to do so. There never was a "Ukrainian question" to add to the European diplomatic agenda together with the Polish, the Czech, and the South Slav "questions."

At a time when other national movements attracted the attention of Europe's intellectuals, Ukraine's seemed mute or part of the larger struggle for the Russia-to-come after the fall of

---

[1] M. Hrushevsky, *The Historical Evolution of the Ukrainian Problem* (London: S.V.U., 1915), p. 51.

3

czarism. Ukraine was a largely peasant and provincial land. "One is struck by the fact," writes the historian Marc Raeff, "that at the moment of its subordination to Muscovite Russia, it was Ukraine that enjoyed and exercised a clear cultural predominance; much later, in the nineteenth century, at the birth of modern national consciousness, Ukraine had the status of a peasant culture adjudged inferior and harshly repressed."[2] The czars sought to keep it that way, banning the printing of all but a handful of books in the Ukrainian language. Only in the first decade of the twentieth century did the Russian Imperial Academy of Sciences admit that Ukrainian was a language and not a dialect of Russian. It is no wonder that for the Western statesmen who gathered at Versailles to redraw the map of Europe, there was no "Ukrainian question."

This general ignorance and neglect of Ukraine by the West continued throughout the Soviet period. Preoccupation with Ukrainian national aspirations was reserved for either émigré circles or Soviet ideological and police forces. Only the imminent collapse of Soviet power brought Ukraine and the other captive nations of the Soviet Union into prominent relief. These nations appeared to many in the West as if from a mist, and, like all ghostly apparitions, they—most of all Ukraine—stirred fear and anxiety. On the very eve of independence, in August 1991, President George Bush traveled to Kiev and delivered what was widely and correctly seen as a warning to Ukraine that " . . . freedom is not the same as independence . . . [Americans] will not aid those who promote a suicidal nationalism based on ethnic hatred."[3] This implicit characterization of Ukraine as a land of "suicidal nationalism" was both impolitic to make in Kiev and just plain wrong. Nationalist organizations were active in the Ukrainian independence movement, but they were hardly the dominant influence in Ukrainian politics. No outburst of nationalism could alone have brought about independence. Rather, from the very beginning, the driving force behind Ukrainian independence was an alliance

---

[2] Marc Raeff, "Ukraine and Imperial Russia: Intellectual and Political Encounters from the Seventeenth to the Nineteenth Century," *Ukraine and Russia in Their Historical Encounter*, eds. Peter J. Potichnyj, Marc Raeff, Jaroslaw Pelenski, and Gleb N. Zekulin (Edmonton, Alberta: Canadian Institute of Ukrainian Studies, 1992), p. 69.

[3] *Remarks by the President in Address to the Supreme Soviet of the Ukrainian Soviet Socialist Republic* (The White House: Office of the Press Secretary), 1 Aug. 1991.

of forces suspicious of Moscow; in addition to nationalists, this alliance included those who sought to insulate Ukraine's relatively higher standard of living from the instability of Moscow, as well as large segments of the leadership of the Ukrainian Communist Party. President Bush's embrace of an image of Ukraine as a land rent by ethnic division fueled other, equally anxious perceptions of Ukraine as a country bent on conflict with Russia, a nuclear renegade, or even a state so torn by inner divisions and turmoil that it could not survive.

The appearance of Ukraine represented a strategic discontinuity *par excellence* that inspired anxiety about an unknown and risky future and recalled Europe's complicated and dangerous past. In light of this anxiety, it is not surprising that the West's first images of Ukraine were characterized by a sharp apprehension about this new state—and all of the former Soviet Union. Despite five years of independence, nuclear disarmament, and the beginnings of economic reform, these images continue to influence Western, and especially European, thinking on Ukraine.

Yet it is as dubious strategically as it may be comforting psychologically to cling to such first reactions, or to try to shoehorn Ukraine and the region as a whole into familiar patterns. It is the thesis of this book that the emergence of an independent Ukraine represents a great departure from the accustomed patterns of political life in Central and Eastern Europe.[4] The old patterns of empire may not be forever vanquished, and the small- and medium-sized nations may not be guaranteed success, but it is clear that the chances for both propositions will be greatly increased if Ukraine remains independent and stable.

How likely is such an outcome? Ukraine's vulnerabilities in 1993 led many observers to see it as a doomed state. Although agreements on nuclear disarmament and the start of economic reform have softened this judgment, many still believe that Ukraine has no alternative but a choice between Russia and the West. In Europe especially, the majority view remains that Ukraine is very different from Poland, and still not a serious can-

---

[4] Throughout this book, "Central and Eastern Europe" designates Belarus, the Czech Republic, Estonia, Hungary, Latvia, Lithuania, Moldova, Poland, Romania, Slovakia, and Ukraine.

didate for the West's main institutions. These doubts about Ukraine's place in Europe are usually linked to the view that Ukraine is somehow Russia's problem. While no one wants a militarily significant redivision of Europe, there are many who believe that a politically and economically significant division is inevitable, and that Ukraine belongs in the East. The term "Finlandization" has even been resurrected to describe a possible "end game" for Ukraine and Russia.

Even in the United States, where appreciation of the strategic significance of an independent Ukraine is much greater than in Western Europe, support for Ukraine has had to overcome two great obstacles. The first was the presence of nuclear weapons on Ukrainian soil, the elimination of which was such an obvious and overwhelming interest of the United States that it brought a high level of political and economic engagement. This level of engagement paid off. The last nuclear warhead left Ukrainian soil in June 1996, and the U.S.–Ukrainian relationship is still riding on momentum generated by this success. The second obstacle is American confusion about the role of the United States in post–Cold War Europe. Many different voices are competing to define this role. Some urge a greater domestic focus; others, a turning away from Europe toward the Pacific. Even among those who stress the continued importance of U.S.–European ties, the vast majority focus on Western Europe or, at best, an expanded NATO. They have yet to grasp the importance of states like Ukraine, Estonia, Latvia, Lithuania, and even Belarus to European stability—particularly if Western security obligations are to be defined by a new front-line on the eastern edge of Poland.

These perceptions and attitudes toward Ukraine, rooted in the past, have potentially serious consequences, since the greatest challenges to a stable security structure in this region of Europe lie ahead. Ukraine has enjoyed an unprecedented freedom from external pressures—a "breathing space" to address the internal challenges of state-building and regime consolidation. But now both Russia and the West are asserting themselves in Central and Eastern Europe. Russia has concluded the latest in a series of agreements with Belarus designed to deepen integration. These agreements include military provisions, which are increasingly discussed as part of an eventual response to NATO expansion. Russia continues to embrace a view of all of the former USSR as a zone of its vital interests appropriately safeguarded by integration among the Soviet successor states. No serious difference of opinion on this issue emerged during the Russian presidential elections. Indeed, President Boris Yeltsin publicly made integration the centerpiece of his campaign by signing two agreements in the spring of 1996 to deepen integration's scope and pace by creating a "Community of Sovereign States" with Belarus and an economic union with Belarus, Kazakhstan, and Kyrgyzstan. NATO is also on the verge of expanding into the region. Ukraine does not fit easily into the security system implied by either Russian or NATO policy, yet its fate is crucial to the shape, costs, and consequences of both.

Ukraine's importance to a secure and stable Europe, obscured for some time by Western concentration on the crucial matter of nuclear disarmament and Kiev's hesitant economic reform, is only now becoming apparent. What has been obvious in Moscow from the very beginning has only slowly dawned on Western observers: Ukraine is the keystone in the arch of the emerging security environment in Central and Eastern Europe. It is a state that is too large and too geographically central to this emerging security environment to be ignored. Key issues of Russia's own long-term evolution are bound up in its relations with Ukraine. Russia's definition of itself as a state and international actor is significantly shaped by its long-term ties with Ukraine. It is a matter of particular importance whether a new era of normal state-to-state relations can replace a long and complicated history of Kiev's subordination to Moscow. Whether Russian-led integration on the territory of the former USSR will pose a serious, long-term military challenge to the West depends in large part on the role that Ukraine plays or is compelled to play within the Commonwealth of Independent States (CIS). As Zbigniew Brzezinski has succinctly stated, "It cannot be stressed strongly enough that without Ukraine, Russia ceases to be an empire, but with Ukraine suborned and then subordinated, Russia automatically becomes an empire."[5] The vulnerability of NATO's new front-line if the Alliance expands also depends in

---

[5] Zbigniew Brzezinski, "The Premature Partnership," *Foreign Affairs*, 72: 2 (Mar.-Apr. 1994), p. 80.

no small measure on Ukraine—both on Ukraine's internal success at stabilization and on its ability to maintain a friendly, engaged neutrality toward the Alliance.

What is needed in the West is analysis of Ukraine and its security policy as a means of fully understanding the potential opportunities and risks that lie ahead. The West cannot afford for Ukraine to remain an "undiscovered" country. This book is intended to fill in some of the gaps that exist in the study of Ukraine and the security environment of the region as a whole.

Chapter 1 analyzes the domestic roots of Ukrainian security policy, particularly the still unfinished task of building a stable state against a diverse ethnic, economic, and regional mix. Ukrainian security policy is wholly bound up with securing independence and establishing a stable and workable domestic consensus that will support that independence. Despite great strides made since 1991, Ukraine continues to face challenges to its stability, including internal divisions, the lack of sustained economic reform, and weaknesses of both political institutions and leadership. The West often exaggerated these challenges in 1993-94 (the period when Ukrainian recalcitrance on nuclear weapons was at its height), concluding that Ukraine might collapse. In fact there are also sources of stability that many analysts underestimated and that to date have been stronger than the disintegrative forces—although Ukraine at the same time continues to be threatened by the concentration of economic and political power in the hands of a few and by the slow progress toward market reforms. The country's future depends on averting economic collapse and external pressures that would give these internal challenges new life.

The rest of this book treats the three main preoccupations of Ukraine's security policy: Russia, Central and Eastern Europe, and the West. All three are closely linked to Ukraine's internal focus on state-building and independence and the dictates of geography and history. All three also relate to maintaining the existing "breathing space" and ensuring a stable region. The West does not directly challenge Ukrainian independence, but policies such as the expansion of NATO could end up placing Ukraine in a "gray zone" or worse. In addition, some form of Western support is crucial for Ukraine if it is to maintain internal reforms and to stabilize its relations with Russia.

Chapters 2 and 3 look at the problem of Ukraine's securing stable relations with Russia, at the basic forces shaping those relations—including the history and psychological attitudes of both sides—and at the key, unfinished topics on the Ukrainian-Russian agenda. This relationship has, against all expectations, maintained a core of great stability and pragmatism—which could, nevertheless, still unravel. Both the parties themselves and the outside world need to work to help create a momentum for the resolution of outstanding issues and the basis for normal, state-to-state ties.

Chapter 4 looks at Ukraine's security environment in Eastern and Central Europe as defined by three major forces: the increasing power of each state in the region to shape its own destiny; the pressure of outside forces; and the states of the region themselves. The reconstitution of Russian power in anything like its former dimension is a problem for the far future, but a possible basis for such a reconstitution is being laid. The chapter focuses on the crucial role that Russian-Belarusian integration could play in the region, both in shaping the security environment and in advancing or slowing down integration among the states that make up the Commonwealth of Independent States (CIS). Ukraine has to be concerned about the after-effects of NATO expansion—particularly about the possibility that it might trigger Russian military countermeasures that would reverse the decade-long trend toward lower levels of nuclear and conventional forces in the region. Ukraine must also deepen its links with Poland, resolve growing problems with Romania, and contribute to the stability of a weak and internally fractured Moldovan state.

Chapter 5 examines the beginnings of Western policy toward Ukraine, reviewing the lessons of the West's pursuit of Ukrainian nuclear disarmament. Chapter 6 looks to the future: it argues that the current momentum that underlies U.S. policy toward Ukraine is a product of the disarmament process and is not yet securely anchored in a coherent definition of U.S. interests in post–Cold War Eurasia. The chapter summarizes why a more comprehensive and vigorous approach is needed and suggests the main elements of a "post-nuclear" U.S. and Western policy toward Ukraine and the region.

Ukraine already plays a much larger role in the security of Europe than either Western commitments or analyses currently reflect. Hrushevsky may have been a poor prophet as to the consequences of denying Ukrainians a state of their own at the beginning of this century, but he offered an apt warning about the consequences of Ukraine's failing to secure a place for itself in Europe today. There is a great difference between the time of the Versailles Treaty and today: the statesmen of the 1920s made decisions that determined which nations would become states and which would remain stateless. Today's diplomats have no such power. The current political geography is not their work, but that of disintegrative forces that unraveled the Soviet Union. Ukraine now has a chance to be the security keystone for this part of Europe; its failure to become that could mean a collapse of peace for Europe as a whole.

CHAPTER 1
DOMESTIC SOURCES OF INSTABILITY AND BALANCE

In 1991, for the second time in this century, an independent Ukraine appeared on the map of Europe. Despite decidedly more favorable external circumstances than those of 1917, the new Ukraine did not look much stronger than its predecessor. Its president frequently warned of the danger of "two Ukraines"—of a split along ethnic and regional lines. Voices in Russia took delight in pronouncing Ukraine "a fragile, artificial, heterogeneous ethno-political formation lacking any real chance for the formation of its own statehood. . . ."[6] Surprised by the collapse of the Soviet Union and unprepared for the emergence of an independent Ukraine, President Bush was not alone in warning of the dangers of "suicidal nationalism." A chorus of analysts noted with alarm the dangers of a nuclear Ukraine. They looked at the economic collapse and hyperinflation, which reached its peak in 1993-94, and concluded that Ukraine would not survive.[7]

Yet Ukraine has survived and taken steps to strengthen itself. In January 1994, Presidents Kravchuk, Yeltsin, and Clinton signed the Trilateral Agreement, bringing to an end Ukraine's flirtation with nuclear weapons. With the nuclear issue out of the way, tentative exploration of Western assistance began. Ukrainian voters chose a new Parliament in March 1994. That summer's Group of Seven (G-7) meeting promised international assistance for Ukrainian economic reform. In July, Leonid Kuchma was elected president and pledged a program of eco-

---

[6] Andranik Migranyan, "Rossiya i blizhnee zarubezh'e," *Nezavisimaya gazeta*, 18 Jan. 1994.
[7] For examples of predictions of Ukraine's imminent collapse, see Daniel Williams and R. Jeffrey Smith, "U.S. Intelligence Sees Economic Plight Leading to Breakup of Ukraine," *The Washington Post*, 25 Jan. 1994; Rowland Evans and Robert Novak, "West Is Still Unsure How to Aid Ukraine," *Chicago Sun-Times*, 9 June 1994; Eugene B. Rumer, "Will Ukraine Return to Russia," *Foreign Policy*, 96 (Fall 1994), pp. 129-144; F. Stephen Larrabee, "Ukraine: Europe's Next Crisis?" *Arms Control Today*, 24:6 (July/Aug. 1994), pp. 14-19.

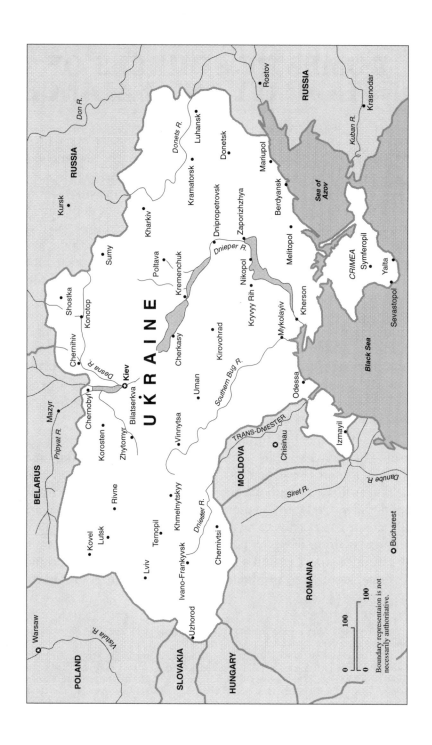

nomic reform and a new pragmatism in dealing with Russia. The transition of power to the new president went without a hitch. In October, Kuchma presented his reform package, winning parliamentary approval. The more important battle for the expanded presidential powers necessary to implement the package soon followed, with Kuchma winning a temporary constitutional arrangement in June 1995 and a new constitution a year later.

These reform measures have been important, but Ukrainian state and social structures also have shown amazing resilience. To those who had predicted Ukraine's collapse, it seemed that Ukraine had dug itself a hole and then found a way out just in time. But something else was also at work. Nearly every step taken in 1994 and 1995 headed Ukraine in a positive direction, yet none of these steps truly transformed the fundamental social, economic, or political conditions that had led so many to conclude that Ukraine was doomed. These conditions are still present—if in a less combustible form than in late 1993.

A "great divide" still separates the "Russian" and "Russified" east from the "Ukrainian" west. Ethnic and regional divisions still challenge the very basis of Ukraine's claim to long-term independence as a single political entity. The political institutions of the state remain unsettled, even after the passage of a new constitution. The state continues to function as if it did not notice the civil society growing up around it. Moreover, a "party of power" runs the state, and some of its members put personal enrichment ahead of national prosperity. Economic change has proceeded in fits and starts, appearing to have generated the necessary momentum only in late 1995 and 1996. But these internal problems have not been matched by external pressures such as those which doomed the Ukrainian Republic earlier in this century. The leaders of today's Ukraine do have a "breathing space" to address the country's problems that their predecessors did not enjoy.

Although most Western and Russian warnings of Ukraine's collapse died away with the emergence of a stable arrangement on nuclear weapons and President Kuchma's economic reform plan, Ukraine is by no means over the tumult and out of danger. Regional and ethnic divisions, economic reversal, and politics at the center still need to be addressed by Ukrainians themselves and understood by outsiders. Perhaps from the very beginning

13

UKRAINE: DISTRIBUTION OF ETHNIC UKRAINIANS AND ETHNIC RUSSIANS

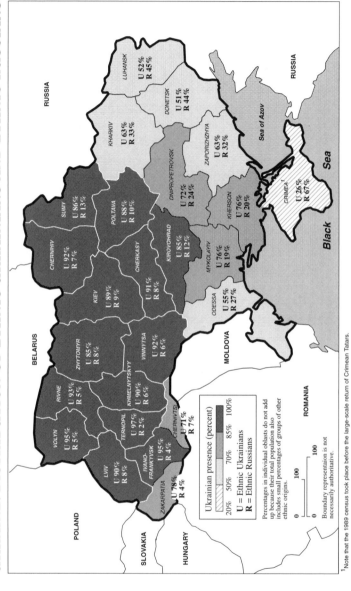

Ukrainian presence (percent)

20% 50% 70% 85% 100%

U = Ethnic Ukrainians
R = Ethnic Russians

Percentages in individual oblasts do not add up because their total population also includes small percentages of groups of other ethnic origins.

0 ———— 100
0 ———— 100

Boundary representation is not necessarily authoritative.

RUSSIA

LUHANSK
U 52%
R 45%

DONETSK
U 51%
R 44%

KHARKIV
U 63%
R 33%

ZAPORIZHZHYA
U 63%
R 32%

DNIPROPETROVSK
U 72%
R 24%

KHERSON
U 76%
R 20%

CRIMEA¹
U 26%
R 67%

Sea of Azov

Black Sea

RUSSIA

SUMY
U 86%
R 13%

POLTAVA
U 88%
R 10%

CHERNIHIV
U 92%
R 7%

CHERKASY
U 91%
R 8%

KIROVOHRAD
U 85%
R 12%

MYKOLAYIV
U 76%
R 19%

ODESSA
U 55%
R 27%

KIEV
U 89%
R 9%

BELARUS

ZHYTOMYR
U 85%
R 8%

VINNYTSA
U 92%
R 6%

RIVNE
U 93%
R 5%

KHMELNYTSKYY
U 90%
R 6%

VOLYN
U 95%
R 5%

TERNOPIL
U 97%
R 2%

IVANO-FRANKIVSK
U 95%
R 4%

LVIV
U 90%
R 8%

ZAKARPATIA
U 78%
R 4%

CHERNIVTSI
U 71%
R 7%

POLAND

SLOVAKIA

HUNGARY

ROMANIA

MOLDOVA

¹Note that the 1989 census took place before the large-scale return of Crimean Tatars.

Source: Data from Taras Kuzio and Andrew Wilson, *Ukraine: Perestroika to Independence* (New York: St. Martin's Press, 1994), p. 30; data is based on the 1989 census of the Soviet Union.

both groups have misunderstood the sources of stability and instability within Ukrainian society. A closer look reveals that they exist, that they continue to play an important role in shaping domestic and foreign policy, and that at least some of the sources of resilience in Ukrainian society crop up in the most unlikely places.

THE "GREAT DIVIDE"

Ukraine's deep ethnic, cultural, and economic faultlines inevitably mold its politics. Ukraine's regions have taken shape under diverse political circumstances, demographic pressures, and even religious orientations. They have distinct histories, so it is no surprise that their inhabitants have different attitudes and outlooks. The Ukrainian leadership has had only a short time in which to build a state out of what had been a diverse and exploited province of the Russian Empire and the Soviet Union. Ethnic, religious, and regional differences are likely to remain at the core of Ukrainian politics for decades to come. They affect nearly every political issue in Ukraine. But do they pose a danger to the state itself? In particular, does a "great divide" between the ethnic Russian and Russified east and the ethnic Ukrainian west threaten the state?

Ethnically, Ukraine is largely Ukrainian. According to the 1989 Soviet census, ethnic Ukrainians make up roughly 73 percent of the total population (over 37.4 million of 51.4 million). Ethnic Russians comprise roughly 22 percent (11.4 million).[8] Only in Crimea do Russians make up the majority, and even there, they are concentrated in the eastern and southern regions. Ethnic Russians account for over 30 percent of the population in Kharkiv, Donetsk, Luhansk, and Zaporizhzhya, and for over 20 percent in Dnipropetrovsk, Kherson, Odessa, and the city of Kiev.[9] In these regions, this presence of ethnic Russians and the political and cultural influence of Russia has deeply affected the language and overall orientation of the majority Ukrainian pop-

---

[8] USSR 1989 census figures are provided in *Natsional'nyi sostav naseleniya SSSR, po dannykh perepisi naseleniia* (Moscow: Finantsy i statistika, 1991). For breakdowns by region, see also F. D. Zastavnyy, *Geografiia Ukrainy* (Lviv: Svit, 1994), pp. 411-417, and the summary table based on the 1989 census in Taras Kuzio and Andrew Wilson, *Ukraine: Perestroika to Independence* (New York: St. Martin's Press, 1994), p. 30.

[9] Kuzio and Wilson, op cit., p. 30.

ulation. Moreover, Moscow has influenced the economic development and settlement patterns of these regions—first under the Romanovs and then under the Soviets—with larger ends in mind than the autonomous development of Ukraine and the people who live there. The question is whether these policies have produced two separate Ukraines.

As Dominique Arel has argued, when one looks at the division within Ukraine on the basis of language of first preference rather than ethnicity, the Russophone population (ethnic Russians and Ukrainians who speak Russian as their language of choice) is more or less equal to the Ukrainophone. From this point of view, the "divide" is even more significant than the census numbers suggest. Moreover, surveys conducted by Arel and his colleagues throughout 1994-95 show a strong correlation between language of preference and positions on key issues such as relations with Russia and the internal structure of the state.[10] These and other surveys have shown marked regional differences on fundamental social issues such as private property and market reform, the preservation of the Russian language, or the need for integration with Russia.

The two most common scenarios translating this division into a threat to the Ukrainian state focus alternatively on the Russian minority and the Ukrainian state itself. The first scenario sees the high concentration of ethnic Russians and Russified Ukrainians as a more or less permanent minority that will grow increasingly separate with time. This community is in itself a source of instability and a potential lever that Russia could use to intervene in Ukraine's domestic affairs. In the second scenario, the danger comes from the Ukrainian side, particularly from a Ukrainian state that finds itself unable to create a genuine political community of these two disparate halves and thus is forced to adopt a more openly ethnic orientation in its state-building practices—choosing to divide the country to save the Ukrainian state.[11]

---

[10] Dominique Arel, "Ukraine: The Temptation of the Nationalizing State," in *Political Culture and Civil Society in Russia and the New States of Eurasia*, ed. Vladimir Tismaneanu (Armonk, New York: M.E. Sharpe, 1995); and Zenovia Sochor, *Political Culture and Foreign Policy: Elections in Ukraine 1994*, Paper No. 76 (College Park, MD: Russian Littoral Project, Univ. of Maryland and Johns Hopkins Univ.–SAIS, Oct. 1994).

[11] On the definition of a nationalizing state, see Roger Brubaker, "National Minorities, Nationalizing States and External Homelands in the New Europe," *Daedalus*, 124:2 (Spring 1995), pp. 107-132.

Concern about the "great divide" preoccupies Ukrainian statesmen. In his July 1994 inaugural address, President Kuchma underscored the potential dangers arising from the ethnic divisions in the country: "[W]e must understand that Ukraine is a multiethnic state. Any attempts to ignore that fact threaten a deep schism and the collapse of the idea of Ukrainian statehood."[12] His predecessor, Leonid Kravchuk, justified key foreign economic and security policies, particularly his compromises on the CIS, as a way of avoiding the emergence of "two Ukraines."[13] The need to ensure balance between different regions and ethnic groups has loomed large on every important political issue in Ukraine from constitutional and legal change to economic reform. In the nuclear debate as well, Ukraine's internal divisions played a decisive role.[14]

Yet demonstrating that ethnic politics and regional divisions play an important role in Ukrainian politics is far from proving that these factors threaten the consolidation of the state. Ethnic politics and regional divisions are a part of stable societies. The weakness of the Ukrainian state and its political traditions magnifies the destabilizing aspects of these factors, but the emphasis on the "great divide" as a potential danger to Ukrainian statehood has led analysts to miss also seeing it and the other divisions within Ukraine as key factors in the *stability* of the state during its most difficult moments. The most important variables for determining whether the great divide will appear and challenge Ukrainian statehood are exogenous to the regional and ethnic divisions themselves, resting particularly with the fate of the Ukrainian economy and Russia's long-term policy toward Ukraine and its Russian minority. The ethnic or ethnolinguistic divide is more a complicating factor than a motive

---

[12] "Leonid Kuchma Takes Oath of Loyalty to the Ukrainian People," *Golos Ukrainy*, 21 July 1994, p. 2.

[13] For example, on the CIS charter and economic union, Kravchuk has spoken of the danger of "the creation of a situation in which Ukrainian society is divided into two defined groups" and of the need to avoid the emergence of "two Ukraines" (*Golos Ukrainy*, 20 Jan. 1993; *FBIS Daily Report: Central Eurasia*, 22 Sept. 1993, pp. 26-27).

[14] On the link between Ukrainian domestic policy (including the ethnic and regional divisions) and nuclear policy, see the author's essay, "The Sources and Conduct of Ukrainian Nuclear Policy: November 1992 to January 1994," in *Nuclear Challenges for Russia and the New States of Eurasia*, ed. George Quester (New York: M.E. Sharpe, 1995), pp. 125-151.

17

force. In the absence of overwhelming economic or external pressures, there are a number of constraints and limitations on the intensification of the "great divide" as a threat to Ukrainian stability. Four of these are explored in the following discussion.

NOT ONE "DIVIDE," BUT MANY

The first constraint is that Ukraine is made up of several important regional, economic, and cultural divisions that cut across the "great divide." The country does not on every issue divide between Russians and Ukrainians, or Russian and Ukrainian speakers, at the Dnieper River. In looking at key social and political attitudes, there are at least five important regional divisions: the eastern, central, southern, and western regions and Crimea. The east includes four oblasts that are the most Russified and highly industrialized: Dnipropetrovsk, Donetsk, Luhansk, and Zaporizhzhya. Crimea is a region unto itself. The west includes the most ethnically conscious Ukrainian regions of Galicia-Volyn (Lviv, Ternopil, Ivano-Frankyvsk, Volyn, and Rivne) as well as Zakarpatia and Bukovyna, which historically have a much looser connection to Ukraine as a whole. The south includes the oblasts of Odessa, Kherson, and Mykolayiv—an area opened up to settlement only after the Russian conquest of Crimea in 1783 and formerly known as Novorossiya. Odessa and other southern oblasts exhibit distinct social and political features, although they are often lumped under the Russian and Russified east. The center includes the remaining, highly diverse oblasts—ranging from Kharkiv in the east to Khmelnytskyy in the west. It would be easy to expand this list by subdividing the center into the east-central and the west-central regions and making Kiev its own region.

The purpose here is not to demonstrate precisely how many ways there are to cut a pie. The literature demonstrates no real consensus on how many politically relevant subdivisions there are. One study finds six.[15] Grigoriy Nemiria, a scholar from Donetsk and the leading student of Ukraine's regions surveys models with as many as eleven.[16] Whatever their actual

---

[15] Evhen Golovakha and Natalya Panina, "Public Opinion in the Regions of Ukraine: the Results of a National Poll," *A Political Portrait of Ukraine*, 5 (1995), p. 7.

[16] Grigoriy Nemiria, "L'état et les regions," *L'autre Europe*, 30-31 (1995), pp. 165-177.

number, the existence of more than two constrains a rift along one "great divide." These regions represent a wide mix of ethnic, cultural, and economic interests.

The sharp differences between eastern and western regions usually garner most of the attention, but the role of the center and, to a lesser extent the south, is instructive. The 1994 presidential elections—though usually cited as proof of the "great divide"—provide a good example. Voting patterns in both rounds demonstrated remarkable geographic divisions. In the second round, ten regions in the east gave Kuchma more than 74 percent of the vote. Seven oblasts in the west gave Kravchuk over 84 percent. But there was also a central belt of eight oblasts where neither candidate received more than 60 percent—what Ukrainian analysts described as "a space of peculiar political ambivalence."[17] It is here that Kuchma won the election and Kravchuk lost it. Though the central region's votes for Kuchma were high by Western standards, they were far below the levels that appeared in either the eastern or the western oblasts. These regions do not fit easily into the stereotypical view of either "half" of Ukraine.

This fact is often overlooked, precisely because the campaign itself exacerbated regional differences and therefore reflected an exaggerated vision of them in the final totals. Kravchuk could hardly run on his record of managing the economy. He chose instead to run as a defender of Ukrainian statehood and cast Kuchma in the role of a dupe of Russia. Kuchma countered by appealing first and foremost to issues of interest to the eastern regions—particularly the establishment of Russian as a second state language and a more business-like relationship with Russia. Although the campaign thus turned on issues that Arel and other scholars have found to be most likely to polarize the Ukrainian polity as a whole, these issues did not in fact split the country. What is also noteworthy is how the ordinary complexities of Ukrainian political life quickly returned to the forefront, even in the eastern and the western regions. The more balanced and regionally diverse forces quickly asserted themselves. Both Kravchuk and Kuchma, whatever their campaign rhetoric,

---

[17] Svitlana Oksamytna and Serhiy Makeev, "Sociological Aspects of Political Geography in Ukraine," *A Political Portrait of Ukraine*, Vol. 5, 1995, p. 2.

ended up broadening their appeal beyond their initial regional strongholds.

The "great divide" could become a dominating influence, given the right circumstances, but at present it is not an all-consuming fact of political life. Other geographic, cultural, and economic divisions supplement this great divide, often serving the cause of political *moderation* by supplying conflicting interests. Extremist political visions of any type are not "saleable" across the whole of Ukraine's diverse political communities. Even within their home regions, such ideas are modified and constrained by the rough and tumble of local politics. At a time of weak central institutions and political traditions, this regional and ethnic diversity creates checks and balances on the political leadership. No extreme view of the state, whether narrowly Ukrainian nationalist or communist integrationist, could triumph under conditions where diverse regions make it difficult to form a solid and stable majority. These divisions force the state to engage in a policy of compromise and moderation.

INTRA-REGIONAL COMPETITION

A second constraint on the "great divide" is a set of internal obstacles within established regions to the emergence and survival of large regional or ethnically based political blocs—especially on the divisive issues that analysts fear would exacerbate basic divisions within Ukrainian society. For example, the eastern regions share concerns about economic, cultural, and political questions at the heart of state-building, but they also must compete politically with one another for scarce political capital. Kuchma's roots in the giant Yuzhmash missile production complex in Dnipropetrovsk appear to have given his former colleagues a head start in winning positions of authority in Kiev. Donetsk and other eastern provinces have done less well in this intra-eastern competition for the spoils of the 1994 elections, although the results were widely seen as a general victory for the east as a whole.

The eastern regions are also economic competitors—for government support as well as for international aid and investment. Notwithstanding the high polling numbers in the east showing a strong bloc in favor of the old economic arrangements, not even a shadow of the old system of mines and heavy industries can be sustained without massive government subsidies. The Ukrainian government cannot afford such an undertaking, as it demonstrated with its tough response to striking miners in February 1996. Inefficient mines and other heavy industry in the east must be closed down if reform is to continue—a trend likely to intensify rather than stifle intra-regional competition. The government must regularly respond to pressures from key interest groups, such as the miners or collective farmers. But even Kravchuk understood the limits of appeasing these interests, particularly after experimenting with massive subsidies in the summer of 1993. Kuchma has adopted a tougher approach, mixed with some "carrots." But the basic condition of the Ukrainian budget, the necessity of sustaining economic reform, and outside pressures from international financial institutions and key Western governments have effectively put an end to hopes that the subsidy pie can be expanded, or that it will be spread widely over the eastern regions.

Electoral politics in the east also does not fly a single flag. In the first round of parliamentary elections in March 1994, it supported a large number of Socialists, Communists, and Agrarian Party candidates, many of whom expressed a desire for integration with Russia.[18] But the east also has been the major basis of support for Russian-language parties favoring economic reforms, including Kuchma's bloc. It has elected innovative regional leaders in Luhansk and Donetsk.[19] Large-scale popular movements for autonomy or secession—like that in Crimea—do not exist. There is no region-wide pattern of strikes or opposition to the government, nor any large-scale movement for the preservation of the Russian language. Strikes or ballot initiatives on the Russian language have been local, not region-wide—despite polling data suggesting widespread regional solidarity.

CONSTRAINTS ON RUSSIA

A third mitigator of the "great divide" is the lack of significant support by the Russian Federation for ethnic and regional political movements within Ukraine. Russia currently enjoys a great

---

[18] On the March 1994 parliamentary elections, see Dominique Arel and Andrew Wilson, "The Ukrainian Parliamentary Elections," *RFE-RL Research Report*, 3:26 (1 July 1994), pp. 6-17.

[19] Iurii Iurov, "Liberal'nyi trykutnyk Donbasu," *Studii politolohichnoho tsentru Heneza*, 1 (1993), pp. 43-52.

deal of eastern sympathy in public opinion polls, but it is in no condition to take on new economic challenges of the size and magnitude desired by Ukraine's Russia-oriented politicians. They and their constituents conceive of a future Russian-Ukrainian relationship largely in old-fashioned terms. Yet experience has shown that leaders in Dnipropetrovsk and Luhansk can do better by playing the regional card in Kiev than by joining the long line for subsidies in Moscow. Integrationist schemes to return to the old prosperity through the restoration of socialist economic ties must confront the fact that Russia's industries are also engaged in a furious competition for scarce resources. The debate within Russia over the defense budget and subsidies for crumbling high-technology industries illustrates that even if the Ministry of Defense wanted to pursue a strategy of military integration with Ukraine, there would be little to spread around to Ukrainian industries.

The great migration of local officials from Dnipropetrovsk to Kiev under President Kuchma provides an example of the power of the state, even in its current condition, to attract the attention and ambitions of key eastern regions. The collapse of the imperial center—and the absence of a strong Russian policy of intervention and support—means that the basic decisions on jobs, honors, resources, and benefits are made in Kiev. The high turnout in the 1994 parliamentary and presidential elections throughout Ukraine (except in the parliamentary elections in Crimea) demonstrates the population's strong orientation toward Kiev. Although some in the east may think of this tie as temporary, there really is no alternative; this orientation alone helps to turn internal divisions from a state-destroying to a state-creating fact of political life. It will never be easy to balance interests in the midst of such ethnic, religious, regional, and economic diversity, but this balancing act is already one of the defining characteristics of Ukrainian politics. The tussle over influence and financial gain among various groups in Kiev is a sign that the state is maturing, not breaking apart.

THE DIRECTION OF UKRAINIAN STATE-BUILDING

A fourth constraint on the threat of the "great divide" to Ukrainian stability is the extent to which the Ukrainian state has successfully addressed and continues to work on the challenges posed by basic divisions within society. The laws, policies, and actions of the Ukrainian government have to date secured the rights of minorities in Ukraine. The basic provisions for citizenship and participation in the country's institutions have been defined from the very beginning in political, not ethnic terms. The combination of this tolerance and the communist-era preeminence of the eastern regions within the Soviet system has meant that ethnic Russians and Russophones from the east have played a preponderant role in the founding and running of the Ukrainian political system. It is they, and not the nationalists of western Ukraine, who run the country. The demographic and industrial weight of the east ensures it will remain an important place in both electoral and informal political calculations. Of even greater importance is the fact that the weight of the east also shapes Ukrainian state-building in fundamental ways.

Ukrainians have never had a state or lived as a political community within anything like the current borders. "The lack of an independent state," as one observer has written, "is an important continuity in Ukrainian history."[20] Ukrainian history is one of a "stateless nation." No one should be surprised if, at first, the internal divisions and other aspects of the Soviet inheritance are stronger than the forces trying to mold a state. As already emphasized, each of Ukraine's regions has a distinct history. Some—particularly the eastern and northern regions of present-day Ukraine—have been subject to centuries-long Russian political control and colonization. In contrast, the western regions of Galicia, Volyn, and Bukovyna were earlier part of other political systems: the Austro-Hungarian Empire, Poland, Romania, and Hungary. During World War II, the Soviet Union absorbed these western regions, and in 1954, Crimea became part of the Ukrainian SSR.

This inheritance places *positive* as well as negative constraints on state-building. No serious Ukrainian statesman who hopes to govern can advocate an ethnic state. The inheritance likewise limits the center's ability to concentrate power, ensuring that the regions have a voice of their own and are players in

---

[20] Gerhard Simon, "Probleme der ukrainischen Staatsbildung," *Aussenpolitik*, 45: 1, p. 61.

Ukrainian political life. Any political scenario that defies these limits must rely either on foreign help or on an internal coup. While such a political scenario can easily be imagined, it is more difficult to visualize how those responsible for seizing power could govern a state like Ukraine over the long-term without an anti-democratic transformation: under ordinary political circumstances, the divisions within Ukrainian society are an effective restraint against extremist politics.

The logic of state-building imposed by this historical tradition is not of the all-or-nothing variety. The choice between Ukraine's re-integration with Russia or a state built on Ukrainian ethnic exclusivity is no choice at all. Nationalism is not the only pillar on which to build a state. Nor is there some inevitable logic that Ukrainian nationalism must emerge as the only glue to hold together a disparate community. Traditional Ukrainian nationalism is too extreme to capture a large number of adherents. Ukraine's diversity forces a remaking of the strategy and ideology of state-building.

This remade ideology will naturally draw upon the majority culture as a building block. A state cannot be constructed against the will of that culture unless it is an authoritarian one. It would be undiscriminating to interpret the government's embrace of Ukrainian as the official language, the emergence of Ukrainian language schools and textbooks, or of ethnic Ukrainian signs and symbols as signs of the dominance of nationalism or of "nationalizing" tendencies in the state. In western Ukraine, the system of subsidies supporting the Russian-language school system and the Russian minority has collapsed. But there is no evidence of any repression of the Russian language or culture. No pattern of discrimination in social life or employment has been discovered.

Ukraine is still a state in the making, and the results could well disappoint both Ukrainian and Russian nationalists. The country might actually succeed in building a state on the historical legacies of diverse settlement and orientation. Ukraine is seeking no special place in the world. It has no exalting mission or great-power aspirations, such as even the most reform-minded Russians believe are essential to a renewed Russia. Thus, to many Russian observers, Ukraine lacks the basic elements that have supported state-building in the Russian tradition. The same Russian observers tend to see the lack of these elements as inevitably leading to fragmentation and failure internally, and thus to Ukraine's "return" to Russia.

The beauty of a strong central state of the Russian type is in the eyes of the beholder. What Ukraine is building is more modest. Its model is more likely to be sought in Poland or the Czech Republic, even though Ukraine lags behind in both political and economic reform. But, in Ukraine as in these states, the nurturing of modest aspirations makes a dominating center less necessary. Ukraine can afford more regional diversity and federalism than can a Russia that seeks a central place in the world. Kiev need not manage every available resource for a larger mission, or control a gargantuan territory. It could not sustain such a project even if it desired to do so. It is a more ordinary state than Russia, and this very ordinariness frees it from constraints that bind its northern neighbor. It can become a state that overcomes its "great divide" without being forced to make the stark choice between ethnic nationalism and integration with the Russian Federation.

Processes already at work in Ukraine are slowly creating a political community that is more than the sum of its parts. Instead of looking for simple expressions of loyalty to Kiev, analysts must understand the multiple and even contradictory sources of attachment to the Ukrainian state beyond language, ethnicity, or culture. Opinion polls show that the number of people favoring Ukrainian independence have continued to climb even as large segments of the population favor integration with Russia.[21] These multiple sources of identification, allegiance, and tolerance range from passionate nationalism to support of the central government's control of political and economic wealth. The test will be whether the Ukrainian state can build upon these multiple and contradictory sources of identification a unifying allegiance to, and tolerance of, the Ukrainian state. The wisdom or good fortune of the Ukrainian government to

---

[21] *Nezavisimaya gazeta*, 1 Mar. 1994, p. 3; and *OMRI Daily Digest*, 10 Jan. 1995. These and other polls seem to capture general moods of satisfaction and dissatisfaction, not deep-seated convictions that are translated into political action. For example, a 1994 poll conducted in 24 Ukrainian regions by the Kiev International Sociological Institute found 40 percent of the respondents expressing preference for Ukraine and Russia being a single state. However, a January 1995 poll by the same organization found 64 percent of Ukrainians polled declaring their support for the country's independence.

date is that it has not pursued policies that bring potential conflicts between those identifications into the open. The "great divide" thus remains a decisive factor in shaping Ukrainian politics, but not a threat of its demise.

This exploration of Ukraine's internal divisions ends with a point that is simple but often overlooked: these divisions—even the "great divide" itself—are not eternal. The distribution of Russophone and Ukrainophone populations is not something established by nature. It came to be as a result of who ruled, who settled where, and how people made their living. The historical circumstances that created the current ethnic and regional divisions have been profoundly disrupted and are unlikely to be reestablished. The forces that Russified ethnic Ukrainians or made Dnipropetrovsk a center of military production have weakened—probably forever. They have little hold over the young. Every year of Ukraine's existence increases the number of its citizens who know little or nothing of the Soviet past. It has been ten years since Mikhail Gorbachev's loosening of the Soviet system and five years since the disappearance of the USSR altogether. Those under thirty know no other existence. Those under forty came of age during the Leonid Brezhnev years and have now spent nearly half of their adult lives under Gorbachev's Soviet Union and in an independent Ukraine. New forces of opportunity and cruel necessity are at work reshaping the Ukrainian polity, and state-building itself is one of these forces. The current political geography of Ukraine must be respected, but it is by no means immutable. It is the task of this generation of Ukrainian statesmen to find a way to build upon the positive legacy of this geography yet create a state and society that is no longer bound by its most serious divisions.

CRIMEA

A potential exception to the above analysis is Crimea. The clearest example of a "great divide" in Ukrainian politics is not between eastern and western Ukraine, but between Crimea and the rest of the country.[22] Crimea is a prime example of a

---

[22] For a broad overview of the Crimean problem, see the essays in Maria Drohobycky, ed., *Crimea: Dynamics, Challenges and Prospects* (Lanham, Maryland: Rowan and Littlefeld, 1995).

world unto itself. Its overt struggle with Kiev over autonomy stands in sharp contrast to the rest of the east. It is the only eastern province in Ukraine with an ethnic Russian majority rather than a majority that is a Russophone mix of ethnic Russians and Ukrainians. The Russian majority in Crimea is of relatively recent origin: most of those who comprise it are post–World War II migrants or their children and grandchildren. Even after becoming part of the Ukrainian SSR in 1954, Crimea remained closely tied to Moscow through its economy, military production, naval bases, and resorts. Local officials retained links with Moscow and, unlike their counterparts in other similarly privileged regions, such as Donetsk and Dnipropetrovsk, were virtually unconnected economically and politically to the Ukrainian SSR. Crimea also hosts Ukraine's only remaining concentration of Russian military force, composed of nearly 40,000 sailors and soldiers associated with the Black Sea Fleet and a large population of military retirees. It is at best a force of divided loyalties with very deep roots in the local Russian community.

These basic factors, unique to Crimea, begin to explain why Crimea has its own politics and political parties and why the question of autonomy (and even independence) has stood at the heart of Crimean politics since early 1992.[23] The election of President Kuchma in 1994 led to a relaxation of tensions that Kiev has skillfully exploited, effectively discrediting Crimean separatism, forcing its legislature to eliminate the Crimean presidency and to bring its constitution into line with Ukraine's own fundamental laws. Fortunately, this dispute has been solely a battle of constitutions and laws, but Crimea remains Ukraine's most serious internal challenge to territorial integrity. Its ethnic divisions, including the Moslem Crimean Tatars, resemble those of the Russian Federation more than those of the rest of Ukraine.[24] Internal questions of autonomy and economic development remain inextricably linked to external ones, such as the status of Russian naval forces of the Black Sea Fleet. Moreover, these external links also include bonds of great sympathy and support,

---

[23] Andrew Wilson, "Presidential and Parliamentary Elections in Ukraine: the Issue of Crimea," in *Crimea: Dynamics, Challenges and Prospects*, ed. Maria Drohobycky (Lanham, MD: Roman & Littlefield, 1995), pp. 107-131; and "Crimea's Political Cauldron," *RFE-RL Research Reports*, 2: 45 (Nov. 12, 1993), pp. 1-8.

[24] Alan Fisher, *Crimean Tatars* (Stanford: Hoover Institution Press, 1978), pp. 165-179.

particularly among the Russian nationalist and Communist parties, which explains part of the reason why President Kuchma and the Ukrainian leadership went out of their way to endorse the reelection of Boris Yeltsin in 1996. The position of Russia and its military assets on the peninsula are strengthened by Ukraine's failure to improve the Crimean economy or to integrate it more closely with the country at large.

The factors that have kept the Crimean problem within manageable limits to date—including Russia's unwillingness to intervene directly in the matter despite its sympathies, Russia's preoccupation with the Chechen crisis, the Ukrainian government's ability to avoid violence and thus to confine the issue to a war of decrees, and the expectations raised by Kuchma's campaign promises and economic reforms—by no means represent a permanent solution. They would all be subject to countervailing pressures if violence erupted on the peninsula between Russians and Crimean Tatars, if the Black Sea Fleet intervened more directly in Crimean affairs (following the example of the 14th Army in Moldova), or if sharp changes affected the political balance of power in either Moscow or Kiev. Crimea's significant economic lag behind the rest of Ukraine—a startling fact in a country where no region has really performed well until recently—creates a further source of tension. A future crisis in Crimea would be a grave secessionist challenge for the Ukrainian government but would not automatically mean a schism of the country as a whole.

THE WEAKNESS OF THE STATE AND ITS GOVERNING CLASS

Some analysts also have perceived the weak Ukrainian state and its inexperienced ruling class as sources of danger to internal stability. This view continues to be especially popular among a broad segment of Russian diplomats, military officers, journalists, and foreign policy analysts who see the internal divisions just discussed as impossible to overcome without a strong central state. These analysts perceive the Ukrainians to be in no position to build such a state. They view the Ukrainians as having only an "artificial nationalism" that would divide the country, not unify it, and as lacking the material resources to build a working economy and strong state institutions. They consider that, in the long run, the population will be attracted either to local ties of region, culture, and language, or to transnational political and economic integration with Russia. Kiev will find itself squeezed between Donetsk or Kharkiv and Moscow.

By definition, state-building is a process that occurs in the absence of a strong state. In Ukraine, political institutions are still not well-defined, despite the adoption of a new constitution in June 1996. Tensions between the executive and legislative branches continue, with both seeking to expand their powers. The lack of resolution of many fundamental questions of governance is not surprising and need not be dangerous. One can well imagine a process that leads beyond the new constitution, settles the question of legislative and executive powers, and defines the relationship of the center to the regions without undercutting the stability of the state itself. Ukrainian politicians have avoided anything like the passionate contest that led in Russia to the violent showdown between president and parliament in October 1993. Ukraine has held two presidential elections and several rounds of parliamentary elections since independence. The new constitution creates the requirement for yet another round of both presidential and legislative elections, as well as the difficult administrative task of reviewing existing laws and regulations to ensure they are compatible with the new fundamental law.[25]

In the near term, however, the weakness of the state grows less out of still unsettled legal or constitutional questions than out of the problem of who is governing and for what ends. An informal "party of power" still makes most of the decisions. The weakness of Ukrainian civil society, particularly of the mechanisms of press and public opinion that must operate in the intervals between elections, means there is no effective constraint on governmental decision. Although the Ukrainian press is becoming more open and sophisticated, it still has relatively little information or influence on governmental decisions. The same can be said of the institutes and analytical centers that have sprouted up in Kiev. It may in fact be one of the characteristics of post-communist states such as Ukraine that, for some time to come, the old state decision-making structures and new forms of civil society and public opinion exist side by side. While the state no

---

[25] Ustina Markus, "New Constitution Largely a Formality," *Transition*, 6 Sept. 1996, pp. 14-15.

longer dominates civil society, civil society has barely begun to stand on its own feet; the press, public opinion, and democratic structures such as elections are not yet much of a force in influencing governmental decisions.

The men who run Ukraine come from the Soviet ruling class, the so-called *nomenklatura*. The biographies of the sitting and former presidents, prime ministers, and key executive-branch and legislative-branch officials show their roots in the large industrial enterprises, the old republic ministries, and the Ukrainian Communist Party.[26] These backgrounds should not be seen as either destiny or indictment, but they do indicate that the Ukrainian independence movement was not simply a collection of nationalist or dissident groups but became co-opted by the former *nomenklatura*. In a situation in which the need for qualified bureaucrats, managers, diplomats, and soldiers was great and the pool from which to choose them was relatively small, it is not surprising that the old provincial ruling class in large measure became the new national ruling class. Presidents Kravchuk and Kuchma brought to power their former associates, friends, politically important patrons, and potential rivals. Such personnel policies are as old as politics itself, but they tend to be corrupting if unlimited by broader social forces of public opinion and the press or by a fixed set of laws and institutions that regulate political life. Without such constraints, politics tends to become increasingly focused on the struggle for position, influence, and wealth, rather than on basic policy options.

Under President Kravchuk, large sections of the former *nomenklatura* were included in the power and spoils of office. Power and influence were distributed across a wide range of regional and sectoral elites, and a rough balance was maintained among these groups. Under President Kuchma—with the beginnings of real reform and thus of the potential to upset the scheme for the distribution of power and control of resources—this cozy era has given way to a struggle among various groups. There has been a mass migration to Kiev of the former *nomenklatura* of Dnipropetrovsk, where Kuchma served as the director of Yuzhmash, the largest missile factory in the former USSR. By one

---

[26] See, for example, the biographical entries for Kuchma, Kravchuk, Marchuk, and Lazarenko in *Khto ie khto v ukrains'kiy politytsi*, Vypusk 2 (Kiev: KIS, 1995).

count, there were over 60 "Dnipropetrovtsy" in the executive branch in April 1995. By mid-1996, there were over 160.[27] They have come to Kiev for a variety of reasons, though they were brought there principally to shore up the President against potential rivals, particularly former Prime Minister Yevhen Marchuk. In May 1996, this group succeeded in ousting Marchuk and replacing him with one of their own, Pavlo Lazarenko. In June, unknown assailants tried to blow up Lazarenko's car on the way to the airport for a visit to Donetsk. The government blamed anti-reformist elements in the Donetsk region, dismissed the regional governor, instituted heightened security measures, and made charges that labor unrest in Donetsk is the result of regional misappropriation of government finances intended for the miners.[28] In putting together the new, post-constitution cabinet, great care was taken, in the words of Lazarenko, to ensure that "government members were selected based on their professional skills, the ability to work, and commitment. A great job has been done to involve all regions of the state. And most of the Ukrainian regions are represented in the government."[29] Lazarenko understands the need to be seen as creating a national government, but even with these personnel reshuffles, the people from Dnipropetrovsk occupy nearly all the senior positions in the government. They also hold important positions in the media, financial institutions, and industrial concerns—the best positions to take advantage of the quickening pace of privatization.

The Dnipropetrovsk group controls the state, but the state is a weak instrument. Thus the great danger posed by their dominance is not a return to authoritarianism, for they are no more venial or less patriotic than any other group, and, as just discussed, the existing regional divisions are a constraint on authoritarian politics at the center. Rather, the dominance of this group upsets the balance of power between old and emerging elites and will very likely bring about a prolonged and distracting struggle between "haves" and "have-nots" within these elites.

---

[27] On the influence of the Dnipropetrovtsy in the Kuchma government, see the articles by Vyacheslav Pikhovshek in *Most*, 46, pp. 1, 4-5 (translated in *FBIS Daily Report: Central Eurasia*, 19 Dec. 1995); and in *Kiyevskie vedomosti*, May 28, 1996, pp. 3-4 (translated in *FBIS Daily Report: Central Eurasia*, 28 May 1996).

[28] *Narodna armiya*, 19 July 1996, pp. 1-2.

[29] *Molod Ukrayiny*, 16 Aug. 1996, p. 1.

Groupings from Donetsk or Poltava want their share. They are willing to stall crucial privatization and other reforms to restore a balance. Disgruntled elites, regional leaders, and elements within the military and security services are likely to join forces with a weak but by no means insignificant civil society and "black economy" to give this group a run for its money. The centrifugal forces of greed, mistrust, and just plain exhaustion will also act on the ruling group itself. There is indeed evidence that such a process is beginning as privatization and other reforms advance, shrinking the pie available for exploitation. Far-reaching social and international problems will also force decisions on this group, compelling them, if they wish to hold on to political power, to come to terms with the key social and political questions of the day. In the near term, however, these conflicts at the top or near-top of the pyramid will probably get worse; in the next year, they are likely to become the dominant thread of Ukrainian politics—with predictably negative consequences for the swift advance of the reform agenda.

THE ECONOMY

In 1993, Ukraine was on the verge of economic shipwreck.[30] Inflation was over 10,000 percent. Production had declined, according to various estimates, by as much as 50 percent since 1990. The budget deficit stood at 20 percent of GDP, and the balance-of-payments deficit was over $3 billion. Ukraine's economy was in worse shape than that of any country of the former Soviet Union not plagued by civil war or regional conflict. Strikes broke out in the east, prompting the government to grant huge subsidies to the miners and other industrial interests. These difficulties threatened Ukraine internally with instability and made it more vulnerable to external pressure. Ukraine remained dependent on Russia for 90 percent of its oil and on Russia and Turkmenistan for 100 percent of its natural gas. Although the

---

[30] The economic statistics for 1993 and 1994 in this section are drawn from an article by the author and Melissa Meeker, "Ukraine, Rising from the Ashes," in *Strategic Survey 1994-1995* (London: Oxford Univ. Press for IISS, 1995), pp. 82-95. The figures for 1995 and early 1996 are from the *Economist Intelligence Unit Report on the Ukrainian Economy*, 6 May 1996. The data on privatization and its problems are from "On the Pillars of Economic Reform in the Ukraine," a Report of the Kiev Office of the World Bank, March 1996.

industrial production decline suppressed demand, Ukraine was still piling up massive debts as it continued to use energy without paying for it.

Yet even these dismal conditions did not drive Ukraine over the brink—though it clearly stood exceedingly close to the edge. Despite the hardship and turmoil, Ukrainians were patient. Strikes were common enough, but they did not produce mass social protest. The government usually dealt with them by acceding to the demands of the strikers and providing subsidies, though not at the levels originally promised. This strategy made for bad economics, but it helped to keep the social peace. A great help to the Ukrainian government during this time was the absence of either a credible alternative source of funds or support from Russia. The average Ukrainian also benefited from unrecorded sources of sustenance. The monthly statistics showed an unrelenting economic decline, but there was a great disparity between the monthly statistics that chronicled Ukraine's ruinous conditions and the rather normal appearance of everyday life. The economic free-fall went on longer than can be explained by hidden stockpiles. Economic and political models do not capture all the forces at work that kept Ukraine afloat. These forces are of mixed origins. Some are part of the old system (subsidies, housing benefits, and access to special goods); others are rooted in old ways of dealing with hardship (barter, black market); and some derive from commercial activity (legal and quasi-legal) that remains outside governmental control. Many Ukrainians supplemented their work for the state with activities in the largely unofficial economy.

Another reason for Ukraine's economic survival has been real economic reform. In October 1994, President Kuchma presented a comprehensive reform plan to Parliament. After a week's debate, it passed by a vote of 231-254. Kuchma's plan contained three elements:

(1) *Financial stabilization* through deep cuts in subsidies, budgetary restraint, the introduction of a national currency, the rationalization of the tax regime with the aim of increasing revenues, and the elimination of stringent export controls to facilitate the flow of trade;

(2) *Privatization* of state-owned enterprises in all sectors except those which hold natural monopolies, with the

33

> privatization of agricultural land and distribution net-
> works, as well as housing, proceeding at a slower rate;
> and
>
> (3) *Price liberalization* on all goods, with gradual increas-
> es in prices on such vital commodities as housing and
> energy.

The plan was sound, and the first steps were taken, particularly in the area of price liberalization. The special price support for energy was eliminated. The government set low targets
for the budget deficit, and the Central Bank stopped issuing
credits. As a result, inflation was dramatically reduced—from 72
percent a month in November 1994 to 5 percent in May 1995—
where it stayed through August. International financial support
allowed Ukraine to begin repaying its energy debt in the fourth
quarter of 1994. The government concluded a $1.5 billion IMF
stand-by agreement in March 1995.

But these reforms faltered in the second half of 1995.
President Kuchma had to divert much energy in the first eight
months after the reforms gained acceptance to winning legal
authority for the powers he needed to implement the plan. In
the summer of 1995, he spoke of the need for a "correction" to
the reforms. The government began issuing credit to the large
industrial enterprises. During this period, large numbers of former industrial managers, especially from Kuchma's old haunts
in Dnipropetrovsk, began to occupy an increasing number of
senior positions in the government. Moreover, large-scale privatization moved forward at a snail's pace. These developments
caused the IMF to suspend the last two *tranches* of a stand-by
loan in January 1996. In April, the IMF canceled the loan altogether after Ukraine overshot its spending target for the first
quarter, despite ongoing negotiations. A new loan of $867 mil-
lion over nine months was concluded in May 1996.

In early 1997, there are as yet no signs of economic growth,
but the rates of decline in GDP and industrial production are
slowing. Real GDP declined by 11.8 percent in 1995—down
from 24.3 percent in 1994. The fall in industrial production also
eased, from 28 percent in 1994 to 11.45 percent in 1995.
Moreover, real incomes rose by 28 percent in 1995—the first
such rise since independence—though they remain low, averag-
ing $45 a month for 1995. Moreover, these official statistics do

not capture the still unmeasured dynamism of the "informal sector" of the economy, estimated by one study to provide the "main source of income for 2.5 million people, including up to 40 percent of youth in urban and border regions." One of the most impressive aspects of the reform package has been its dramatic reduction of inflation, from a high of over 10,000 percent in 1993 to 180 percent in 1995. The inflation rate was 39.7 percent at the end of 1996 and is forecasted to fall to 30 percent by the end of 1997.[31] A new currency, the *hryvnia*, was introduced in September 1996, accompanied by encouraging signs that the reforms to date have started to pay off.

Privatization is moving forward, though not as swiftly or as comprehensively as it should. During the final quarter of 1995, 8,200 enterprises were privatized, with an additional 5,104 small and 941 medium and large-scale enterprises privatized during the first quarter of 1996. These overall figures, while promising, conceal real problems with the program. In many cases, the state is still the majority or largest shareholder. Foreign participation in the plan remains low—a result of Ukraine's political instability, the forest of communist-era regulations, high taxes, and a tangled bureaucracy. Voucher privatization has reached slightly more than half of all Ukrainians—with only 28 million receiving vouchers by the end of 1995, and only 15 million recipients using vouchers to acquire shares. Opposition to privatization, particularly in Communist and Socialist-dominated strongholds in the eastern part of the country, remains strong.

The big step in price liberalization came with a broad price deregulation in November 1994. Prices for rents, household energy, communal transportation, and other key public services have been raised, but more gradually, and they remain subject to state controls. The state continues to play too large a role in the economy. State spending accounted for more than half (52.5 percent) of GDP in 1995, though this represents a drop from 60 percent in 1994. The state at the federal and regional level maintains a host of anti-market regulations, tariffs, and controls that help to fuel crime and corruption. The problem is less those who have dared to make a living outside the law in the black and

---

[31] "Ukraine: Outlook for 1997-98," *Economist Intelligence Unit Country Reports* (Lexis-Nexis online database), January 28, 1997.

gray markets than those, particularly government officials, who continue to make their living from exploiting the loopholes and special privileges and "back doors" in the current system.

With no dramatic economic downturn in sight, the key task now appears to be lessening the pain that the transition has imposed on large segments of the population, particularly in the east, and ensuring that the changes brought about by reform are perceived as fair. As in Russia, the battle over control and outright ownership of state resources remains at the center of elite politics in Ukraine. Although decisions on these matters are made behind closed doors, it is clear that the continued power of the old *nomenklatura* will distort privatization of large-scale enterprises, energy policy, and foreign trade. Much money has been made by those who have had access to both resources at below market prices and the means to make those resources available on the world market. Just such a scheme apparently financed the exile retirement of former Prime Minister Yukhym Zviahilskyy. Economic reform lessens the opportunities for this kind of large-scale manipulation of reform, but such opportunities for corruption remain a part of Ukrainian political life.

CONCLUSION

Whether one looks at its ethnic and regional divisions, politics, or economics, Ukraine appears far more resilient than many expected in the midst of 1993. The dangers posed by these internal challenges clearly were and remain real, but the sources of stability in Ukraine were stronger and more varied than many predicted. This greater stability does not, however, mean that the work of state-building is done, or that success is foreordained. If one thinks in terms of the threats to Ukrainian statehood in 1917-21, particularly the extraordinary external pressures of Red, White, and German forces, it becomes clear that the Ukrainian state has not yet been put under the kind of stress that could break it—however serious the situation was in 1993-94. Ethnicity and regional diversity, the weak state, and short-sighted leadership are all more likely to be factors that deepen a future crisis than its direct causes. Only a sudden and deep economic downturn would provide an internal equivalent of the pressures of foreign armies.

The scenarios that *could* present serious challenges to Ukrainian stability are to be found elsewhere. Clearly the most worrisome for Ukraine are those that would exacerbate the regional, ethnic, and economic divisions, leading to violence or overwhelming the weak and inexperienced government. Almost all of these scenarios depend upon an external catalyst to get them started, to keep them moving, or to prevent recovery. The four scenarios set out below would place Ukraine's current stability under great stress.

A first such scenario is a crisis in Crimea leading to sustained violence between locals and the Ukrainian army or internal security forces. To date, the central government has managed to contain the dialogue with Simferopol within the confines of a debate over constitutional rights and obligations. Yet the issue is by no means resolved. Local forces could arm themselves, as they have in areas of conflict throughout the former Soviet Union, by the active support or the disorganization of the near-by Black Sea Fleet. Violence might begin between local secessionist paramilitary groups and Crimean Tatars, forcing Kiev to intervene. Ukraine's military and internal security forces would be sorely tested by such an intervention, as would the capacity of the government to contain the violence.

A second scenario is a lurch toward authoritarian politics in Ukraine. Under current circumstances, such a government would not be the result of elections or a consensus within the ruling circles. It would have to arise as the result of a *coup d'état*—perhaps a conspiracy of a small number of nationalist-oriented army or internal security officers. If such a regime appealed to narrow ethnic nationalism for support, it could transform the ethnic divisions within Ukraine in ways that would almost certainly overcome the current obstacles to a united movement of ethnic Russians. A regime of this type would probably be short-lived, given the divisions within the country and the weakness of the state's coercive institutions, but it would fragment Ukraine.

A third scenario is a governmental collapse resulting from catastrophic economic failure. The current reforms are going well, but they are not yet irreversible; the unemployment and social consequences of real change have not even begun; and economic life is not on a secure enough footing to cope with natural or man-made catastrophes.

37

The fourth scenario is an external challenge from Russia. The Russian government might decide to exert greater pressure on, or intervene directly in, Ukrainian affairs. Such a policy might focus on the ethnic Russians, actively encouraging secessionist or other ethnic Russian movements within Ukraine. Russia could also decide to take advantage of any of the above scenarios, decisively altering their character by intervening either on the side of co-ethnics or, in the economic scenario, by supporting the Ukrainian state in return for concessions on integration in the CIS or other Russian-led political, economic, and security structures.

Although current trends lead away from such outcomes, none of the above scenarios is implausible. Ethnic violence and the potential intervention of armed units of the Black Sea Fleet remain possible outcomes of a misstep in Crimea. Ultranationalist elements exist within the armed forces and internal security institutions. Ukraine faces serious economic hurdles. Russia has consistently moved to a more nationalist and assertive position, even though the capabilities to support such rhetoric are lacking. A change in the leadership in Russia could well change the calculus of gains and losses that currently constrains Russia's policy toward Ukraine. Even the early stages of these scenarios would create demands that exceed the Ukrainian government's resources and administrative capacity to cope, thereby creating chaos at the center and encouraging centrifugal forces within the country. The breakdown of central control and the threat it would pose to the Ukrainian state would cause a serious regional crisis. Failed states are rarely good neighbors.

There remain those who would play down the significance of any crises in Ukraine because they believe Ukraine's failure automatically becomes Russia's problem. One analyst has characterized this approach in the following terms: "All Russia has to do is to open its arms and in no time Ukraine can be integrated into Russia again."[32] Yet Russia could not now play this role. Ukraine is a large and diverse country. Intervention in its affairs would be a huge political, economic, and military undertaking. More sober voices in Russia and elsewhere point to the costs and problems of managing Ukraine's collapse. An *Anschluss* would

---

[32] *Nezavisimaya gazeta*, 19 Mar. 1994.

require a massive military operation to keep or restore order—something that is beyond the capabilities of the Russian military today. Even a limited operation designed to control a key region or crucial national infrastructure such as pipelines or communications—or, as was discussed in 1992-93, to reassert control over nuclear sites—would require forces well beyond Russia's capacity. Such an intervention scenario presupposes the support or at least the passivity of the local population—something that could not be counted on throughout Ukraine.

For Russia, the main problem is that intervention in Ukraine under any scenario would require the assumption of enormous political, military, and economic burdens. The economic costs of supporting even a willing Ukraine would be staggering. Russia's own economic and political reforms could not now bear such a burden. A Russian intervention in a collapsing Ukraine would be likely to escalate the crisis, not to resolve it. Ukraine's internal divisions could well become a serious problem under stress. If Ukraine unraveled, the most likely scenario would be the rise of regional fiefdoms. At least some of these would be dominated by extreme nationalists, Russian or Ukrainian; others, by old-style regional party bosses and managers. Some might control the military forces on their territory; others might raise forces of their own. Nearly all such fiefdoms would have their own indigenous defense and industrial facilities that rogue states would see as a source of military technology or know-how. There could be many Ukraines, not just one. None of these successor regions would be as stable internally—or as moderate in its policy toward Russia, Poland, or the region at large—as the current configuration of the Ukrainian state.

Only the prospect of a divided Ukraine would raise the specter of "suicidal nationalism" or violence among ethnic and regional communities on a grand scale. The effect of such a breakdown within Ukraine on the stability of the region is predictable. Waves of refugees and the spill-over from local conflicts would overwhelm the fledgling regimes of East Central Europe. The United States, Western Europe, and Russia would be dragged into an intractable situation. No better illustration exists of the value of Ukrainian independence than thinking through its unraveling.

CHAPTER 2
UKRAINIAN-RUSSIAN RELATIONS: AN OVERVIEW

UKRAINE'S RUSSIA PROBLEM

For Ukraine, Russia will remain a foreign policy priority beyond the current environment of internal distractions and constraints on external power. Russian power has affected the Ukrainian nation and lands throughout much of their history. The link between Ukrainian-Russian state relations and ethnic relations inside Ukraine is also of long-term significance. Ukraine's "breathing space" depends on Russian policy and actions more than on any other external factor. Russia represents a peculiar blend of necessary partner and potential foe. It has consistently provided a relatively stable, though reduced, energy supply despite Ukraine's erratic payment history. It has shown restraint over its actions in Crimea, though not always over its rhetoric. But many Russian leaders resent Ukrainian defiance of Russian policies, and some in Russia favor the direct subordination of parts or all of Ukraine.

The course of the Ukrainian-Russian relationship has not been smooth, but neither armed conflict nor wholesale absorption of Ukraine by Russia is in the offing, as some analysts predicted in 1993-94. The two sides have worked for five years on a long and difficult agenda of issues relating to both the legacy of the breakup of the USSR and the contours of future state-to-state relations. That agenda includes the division of the military assets of the former Soviet Union, nuclear arms, and the Black Sea Fleet; the problems of energy supply and debt; the evolution of the CIS and of other mechanisms for integration on the territory of the former USSR; and a friendship treaty that would resolve outstanding differences over borders and place relations on a new legal basis. Some genuine progress has been made, especially on nuclear disarmament. With IMF prodding,

Ukraine's debt was renegotiated in 1995. Numerous practical questions have been handled in ways that at least suggest the commitment of both sides to developing strong and stable mechanisms for their resolution. In other areas, however, agreement has been difficult. The two sides have divided and redivided the Black Sea Fleet numerous times only to founder on basing and other issues. The signing of the Treaty on Friendship and Cooperation, paired with a visit by President Yeltsin to Kiev, has been "imminent" since 1993, but always delayed—most recently in October 1996.

Yet trends within Russia challenge the continuation of restrained "pragmatism" with Ukraine. The debt agreement in the spring of 1995 called forth strong protests in Russia from those who believe that what was needed was more "stick" and less "carrot." President Yeltsin, who in previous years had played a role of pragmatist and conciliator in Russian-Ukrainian relations, publicly expressed his impatience with Ukrainian policies on the CIS, the Black Sea Fleet, and other matters. Russian policy-makers and analysts indicated frustration that Kiev had answered Russian generosity with nothing but the same refusal to integrate. The 1996 presidential election in Russia further strained Russian-Ukrainian ties; Kiev early and often expressed its preference for Yeltsin, fearing that a Communist victory in Russia would embolden the Communist and Leftist forces in Ukraine. For Yeltsin, however, the election season created additional pressure for tough talk; in April 1996, he postponed a scheduled trip to Kiev, clearly heeding those advisors who looked upon a Russian-Ukrainian summit that did not yield concessions from Kiev as a political liability. In October 1996, Russia imposed a 20 percent value added tax (VAT) on Ukrainian goods. The two sides announced a breakthrough on the Black Sea Fleet at the end of October, which again promptly fell apart. In January 1997, President Kuchma warned of a "deterioration" in bilateral relations.[33] Most observers nevertheless believe that the current troubles are just another low point in a continuing cycle of relations that falls short of normalization but avoids serious conflict.

---

[33] Reuters, 17 Jan. 1997.

INTERNAL DISTRACTIONS AND CONSTRAINTS ON POWER

Any attempt to assess the problems and prospects of Ukrainian-Russian relations must first of all note the constraints that presently limit the ambitions of both powers and together assure the stability of Ukrainian-Russian relations in the short term. Both sides are burdened with the consequences of the collapse of the former political and economic structures and the task of creating a stable system in its place. In Russia's case, there is the additional constraint of a wide-ranging international agenda beyond Ukraine and diminished means to respond to it.

The overarching goal of Ukraine's foreign and security policy is a defensive one: to preserve a favorable external situation that supports, or at least does not interfere with, state-building and internal consolidation. To complete these tasks, Ukraine needs time. The Ukrainian leadership wants to devote scarce resources to internal challenges, not to fending off external foes or to managing spill-over from a regional crisis. The current circumstances may be the most favorable ones for state-building that Ukraine has ever seen, but they are hardly immutable; Ukraine's foreign policy must focus on the preservation of the current "breathing space." Being a potentially middle-level power, but currently a weak state, it does not have the means to oppose or appease its enemies or to entice its friends. The first chapter of this book provided a detailed overview of the ethnic, regional, economic, and political obstacles that dominate the attention of the Ukrainian leadership and make the settlement of outstanding issues with Russia so important. These same problems rob that leadership of the means to reach such settlement.

Russia faces much the same dilemma. Of course, if all of Russia's assets could be marshaled to the Ukrainian issue, and if Russia's external environment permitted such a concentration, there would be no question of Russia's superiority in any of the key categories of state power. It is just such a static analysis of the respective strengths and weaknesses of the two states that inspired the scenarios of Russian military or energy pressure leading to Ukrainian capitulation or collapse. President Yeltsin's reelection in July 1996 put an end to fears of the reemergence of a Communist-run Russia, but it hardly resolved the basic problems that constrain the making and implementation of Russian foreign policy.

There is no denying that an increasingly assertive and nationalist consensus has emerged in Russian foreign policy.[34] Russia's leading statesmen want Russia to remain a "great power" and to deepen integrative trends on the territory of the former USSR. But they face considerable constraints, leading to the possibility that what is likely to be most troubling about Eurasia in the next decade is not Russian strength, but Russian weakness.

Chief among the trends limiting Russian power is the weakness of the Russian state and the fragmentation of executive power—in part the result of the disintegration of the Soviet Union. However, even reform breeds weakness, distraction, and demand for resources that are inconsistent with a strong foreign policy. Individual ministries have nearly sovereign rights in their areas of competence. The president and his closest advisors have regularly responded by creating mechanisms for executive oversight that generate a spate of stories in the West about the reconcentration of power but fail to gain any headway in making sense of this policy chaos.

In making and implementing foreign policy, the government must also cope with new players. Imperial and Soviet foreign policy–making was a highly centralized affair, with power concentrated in the hands of the leader and a few key ministers or advisors. In Russia today, there are many more players of relevance outside the central government. Chief among these are financial and banking interests, the oil and gas sector, and regional elites.

Economics now plays a large part in Russian foreign policy. The government must guard its purse to keep the confidence of the international financial institutions. In formulating foreign policy, it must take into account the need to sustain its internal economic development or to soften the blow of competitive mar-

---

[31] See, for example, Leon Aron's essay, "The Emergent Priorities of Russian Foreign Policy," *The Emergence of Russian Foreign Policy*, eds. Leon Aron and Kenneth M. Jensen (Washington: United States Institute of Peace, 1994), pp. 17-34, esp. pp. 25-30. The Russian consensus on integration is not, however, as solid as it appears. See Sherman W. Garnett, "The Integrationist Temptation," *The Washington Quarterly*, 18:2 (Spring 1995), pp. 35-44.

ket forces on key industries. Moreover, Russian banks, industrial firms, and raw-material producers have foreign economic interests that must be addressed. This "return of economics" recalls the late imperial period, when a mix of economic considerations—ranging from internal industrial and railroad expansion to economic imperialism in the Far East—played a leading role in Russian foreign policy.

Finally, in an unaccustomed role, Russia has largely withdrawn from the wider world as an active player to concentrate its energies on the new countries of the former USSR and adjacent states. The opportunities and risks ahead in Eurasia are bound up with a radical shift from a continent centered on a strong imperial center attempting to expand its power outward to potentially stronger large and middle-sized states on the rim asserting their power toward the center. The zone of new and re-established states no longer under Moscow's control demonstrates a startling change in Eurasia. Moreover, there is growing economic, political, and military intrusion by the states on the outer rim of Eurasia into what was previously the Soviet sphere of influence or even the Soviet Union itself. This intrusion has the potential to substantially alter both regional and continental balances of power. Russia is seeking to derail this process by supporting integration among the new states, but it plainly cannot dominate these border lands as it once did.

The core dilemma of Russian foreign policy thus is the tension between its stated goals and its capabilities—the lack of coherence between its vision of the future security environment in Eurasia and actual developments.

BASIC FACTORS IN UKRAINIAN-RUSSIAN RELATIONS

Some analysts argue that psychological factors, particularly the issue of whether or not Russians accept Ukrainian independence, are decisive for the character of Ukrainian-Russian relations.[35] In April 1995, a key Yeltsin advisor, Dmitri Ryurikov,

---

[35] Roman Solchanyk, "Ukraine: The Domestic and Foreign Policy Agenda," in *U.S. Relations with Russia, Ukraine and Eastern Europe*, Seventeenth Conference, Aug. 24- Sept. 1, 1995, Congressional Program, 10: 4 (Washington, DC: The Aspen Institute, 1995), p. 39.

saw the "attitude of Ukrainian authorities toward Russia" as the key stumbling block to progress on outstanding issues. The Ukrainians, Ryurikov argued, were attempting to build a state "on rejecting specific relations with Russia." Russia has been generous, he argued. After all, "Crimea belonged to Russia" as a matter of history, yet Russia sought compromise. The solution was for Ukraine to adopt "kind, fraternal Slavic compromise" on issues such as the Black Sea Fleet, and the tensions would disappear.[36]

Responding to Ryurikov, former Kuchma advisor and foreign policy analyst Dmytro Vydrin also placed great emphasis on the attitudes shaping Ukrainian-Russian relations. "It is the form of the negotiating process that is currently making me feel somewhat uncomfortable, since, in my opinion, it reflects not Ukrainian-Russian relations, but rather Ukrainian-Moscow relations." Vydrin characterized the style of the Russian negotiators as showing "Moscow official elite" arrogance toward those they perceive as "provincials."[37] No observer of the Ukrainian-Russian relationship could fail to see the importance of this psychological layer and of the complicated historical experience that produced it.

Russia has played the decisive external role in Ukrainian history. A state based in Moscow has dominated Ukrainian lands, in whole or in part, since the mid-seventeenth century. It was Moscow that gathered together the territory that now forms Ukraine, bringing Hapsburg-, Polish-, Hungarian- and Romanian-controlled territory into the Ukrainian SSR. This consolidation of Ukraine had little to do with a regard for the aspirations of the Ukrainian people and much to do with Russia's centuries-old perception of its patrimony over the whole of what is now Ukraine and Belarus. There is in fact an almost perfect correlation between a strong Russian state and Ukrainian statelessness—although Russia is hardly the only power in the region that has regarded Ukrainian national aspirations as illegitimate and destabilizing.

The two peoples have lived side by side for centuries, bound by mutual ties of religion, powerful cultural influences

---

[36] *Kievskie vedomosti*, 28 Apr. 1995, p. 4.
[37] Ibid., 5 May 1995, p. 3.

that flowed back and forth between Kiev and Moscow, and large areas of mixed settlement and intermarriage. But these bonds developed within a political structure of subordination of Ukrainian territory and people to Moscow. As manifestations of Ukrainian nationalism in language, religion, culture, or politics appeared, they were not tolerated. Publication in the Ukrainian language was almost completely suppressed by Alexander II.[38] Ukrainian political aspirations flourished underground, in Galicia—a freer but by no means free region outside Moscow's control—or came out into the open in times of the regime's internal weakness and reform, as in 1905.

This pattern continued under the Soviets, after Ukraine's unsuccessful effort at independence in 1917-21. For the Soviet state, the 1920s were a period of forced consolidation—and even appropriation of non-Russian culture into a Soviet framework. When Stalin inflicted collectivization and famine, between 3 million and 6 million Ukrainians died as a result.[39] The great purges brought more suffering. The USSR absorbed western Ukraine at the beginning of World War II; partisan warfare there lasted into the early 1950s. Soviet rule also profoundly affected the basic demographics and economic structure of Ukraine, bringing waves of industrialization, urbanization, and Russian immigration.

Yet another background element should be emphasized: although Moscow has consistently suppressed manifestations of political defiance in Ukraine, it has just as consistently co-opted those with political and economic skills. At a conference in Kiev in 1994, former Crimean Prime Minister Yevgeni Saburov likened Moscow to a great vacuum cleaner, sucking up all the talent from Ukraine and other Soviet republics. For Ukrainians with skills and education, work in Moscow represented an attractive alternative to life in the provinces.

Most of the senior officials on both sides of the table share a common language and experiences in Soviet political culture. They have the habits of working together within the old system.

---

[38] Hugh Seton-Watson, *The Decline of Imperial Russia 1854-1914* (New York: Praeger, 1967), pp. 81-82, 190-191.

[39] Robert Conquest, *The Harvest of Sorrow. Soviet Collectivization and the Terror-Famine* (New York: Oxford University Press, 1986); and Orest Subtelny, *Ukraine: A History* (Toronto: University of Toronto, 1988), pp. 413-416.

They also have a superficial familiarity with one another that stands in the way of serious study of Ukraine as an independent country.[40] In the institutes where policy analysis is conducted, Ukrainian periodicals and other publications (like those relating to other now independent republics) are scarce. Funding for research travel is inadequate. Many Ukraine analysts in Moscow also undervalue the importance of reading Ukrainian. There is a disturbing tendency among Russian analysts of Ukraine to rely on relatives and family connections in Ukraine—cousins, mothers, or fathers-in-law—as their sources of information and judgments about the Ukrainian state or economy. In Ukraine, for different reasons, there is a similar lack of serious study of Russia, although the Ukrainians derive some advantage from their obligatory familiarity with the Russian language and culture; they read Russian and are used to paying attention to what goes on in Moscow.

This mixed inheritance helps explain the shifts that have marked the Ukraine-Russia relationship: harsh words and threats followed by pragmatism and pledges of new beginnings, followed by new frictions. Outsiders often focus on one or another aspect of this cycle, predicting a "return" to partnership or a Russian-Ukrainian conflict, but in fact the whole has to be analyzed together. Both sides tend to play up stereotypes: Ukrainian statesmen usually remind interlocutors that Russians can "never" accept Ukrainian independence; Russians often claim that Ukrainian actions are predicated on "a defiance of Russia," not genuine interests. The issues under negotiation are in themselves difficult, and the legacy of the past and the psychological dynamics of the present complicate them enormously.

Certain constants in the relationship play an equal or even greater role. The first is the basic disparity of power between the two states. In the long run, Russia is a state capable of wielding much greater political, economic, and military power than Ukraine. The relative gap between Russian and Ukrainian polit-

---

[40] The assessments presented in this section are based on interviews and conversations with Russian specialists on Ukrainian affairs conducted by the author 4-6 times a year since 1994, as well as on the several seminars in Moscow and Kiev that the Carnegie Moscow Center has devoted to Ukraine and Russian-Ukrainian relations over the same period.

ical, economic, and military power at present may be as narrow as it has ever been, despite Ukrainian weakness, simply because of Russia's own internal preoccupations and challenges. As the two states stabilize, this gap will again grow. The most dangerous period in Ukrainian-Russian relations may well lie ahead. The character of this future relationship depends on ambitions and patterns of behavior now being established, and on the success or failure of efforts in both countries to transform their political and economic systems. But under almost any future scenario imaginable, coping with Russia and Russian power will remain a core element of Ukrainian foreign policy.

Russia has vital interests in Ukraine—interests that are not just a matter of nostalgia for past influence or habit but that grow out of Ukraine's key strategic location on the Black Sea and partly astride Russia's links with Central and Western Europe. Russia could not look with indifference upon a Ukrainian alliance with a Western power. Ukraine's crucial geographic location and industrial and other resources make it a pivotal state for an expansionist Russian policy to seek to dominate and for opponents of such a policy to keep out of Russia's control. Ukraine is also a key factor in other issues of vital importance to Russia. The eventual character of the CIS and of integration throughout the former Soviet Union will be determined in large part by Ukraine's willingness—or unwillingness—to participate.

Ukraine has equally vital interests in Russia—particularly in Russia's transformation and stability. Ukraine wants to foster strong ties with Russia. It supports the political and economic transformation in Russia as a key element in regional stability, but it also has an interest in encouraging counterbalances to Russian ambitions. But Ukraine—or even a regional combination of states including Ukraine—cannot alone provide such a counterbalance.

RUSSIAN AND UKRAINIAN PERSPECTIVES ON THE RELATIONSHIP

Among Russian policy-makers, there are at least three sets of views about Ukraine. These orientations shade into one another, but are roughly characterizable as nationalist, accommodationist, and integrationist. The integrationist school has become so popular that it now represents a consensus view on all of the former USSR in general and on Ukraine in particular. Given the basic differences that divide each orientation over tactics and the centrifugal tendencies that still shape the new states of the former USSR, it is best to remain what taxonomists call a "splitter," not a "lumper," in describing conflicting streams of foreign policy thinking in Russia.

The Russian *nationalist* perspective holds that at least parts of current Ukrainian territory belong to Russia for ethnic, cultural, and historical reasons. At various times, such figures as former Vice President Aleksandr Rutskoy or Aleksandr Solzhenitsyn have identified regions of Ukraine that should or will "return to Russia." Some adherents to the nationalist orientation have focused exclusively on Crimea or Sevastopol, arguing that the sole reason Crimea is Ukrainian is Nikita Khrushchev's 1954 "gift" of the peninsula to the Ukrainian SSR. Some focus more broadly on the eastern and the southern regions of Ukraine, which have the largest concentration of ethnic Russians or historical patterns of settlement by Russia.[41] The nationalists focus narrowly on ethnic, historical, or linguistic claims and bestow a grudging legitimacy on Ukrainian aspirations for a state of their own in whatever rump territory lies outside their particular view of a "greater Russia." At the extreme fringe of the nationalist viewpoint, there are those who question the legitimacy of any Russian-Ukrainian ethnic divide at all, preferring to underscore the unity of "Orthodox Rus" civilization. This approach belittles modern Ukrainian nationalism as "narrow and artificial" or geographically limited to western Ukraine.[42] Proponents of this Russian nationalist view have little influence at present, but many of their themes—particularly the "Russianness" of Crimea—frequently crop up in official Russian

---

[41] On November 17, 1992, then Russian Vice President Aleksandr Rutskoy predicted the eventual return of Crimea to Russia. Solzhenitsyn has championed the idea of a unified "Rus," including Russia, Ukraine, Belarus, and parts of Kazakhstan. However, he was also an early proponent of redrawing the existing boundaries in the event of a separation, stating that "only local populations [should] determine the fate of a particular locality." A. Solzhenitsyn, *Rebuilding Russia*, New York: Farrar, Straus and Giroux, 1991, pp. 8-9, 18. See also Solzhenitsyn's exchange of letters on this topic with Vladimir Lukin in *Literaturnaya gazeta*, 1 Apr. 1992.

[42] For a defense of the notions of "Orthodox-Rus" civilization and the "artificiality" of states like Ukraine, see, for example, Natalya Narochnitskaya, "Russia— Neither East Nor West," in *Mezhdunarodnaya zhizn'*, 9 (Sept. 1993), pp. 44-45.

discourse. The Crimean themes strike deep chords in the Russian military, particularly the Navy. A considerable dose of nationalist questioning of the legitimacy of Ukrainian aspirations is also part of more mainstream Russian perspectives on Ukraine. In particular, the strategic rationale for long-term integration plays heavily on the notion that among Russians, Ukrainians, and Belarusians, the ethnic and political walls are not and should not be as high as between these nations and the outside world.

Russian policy-makers of the *accommodationist* school accept the reality of Ukrainian statehood and emphasize the dire consequences of an aggressive Russian policy toward that state. Like the Russian nationalists, the accommodationists want long-term reconciliation between Russia and Ukraine, but they are content to see reconciliation take place within ordinary state-to-state relations. They have tended to focus on the benefits of stability and economic cooperation. The adherents to this view have not been more sympathetic to the substance of Ukrainian positions on the Black Sea Fleet or on debt relief; they simply see the advantage of resolving these questions on an ordinary state-to-state basis. In large part, these advantages derive from a view of longer-term Russian interests, particularly an understanding of the consequences of adjusting boundaries or of sustaining Ukraine in a serious internal crisis. Although some accommodationist themes have also drifted into the integrationist view—particularly among "soft" integrationists, who believe new structures of cooperation are compatible with independent neighbors—the accommodatist stance is mainly confined to the reformist camp, and particularly to economists within it. Russian business and economic interests seeking to take profits, not geopolitical advantage, are also by nature accommodationist. They do not want their individual schemes dependent on the realization of some broader political and social structure.

At present, the integrationist perspective is the strongest among Russian policy-makers. Many diverse and conflicting approaches are united under this banner. Some respect the notion of Ukrainian sovereignty and would try to coax Ukraine into deepening its economic, political, and security ties with Russia. Others see "the restoration of the union of the former Soviet peoples—based on voluntary association—as a historical necessity dictated by Russia's needs and those of world security."[43] Still others are convinced that what is a "breathing space" for Ukraine will in the end turn out to be an aberration; Ukraine will, they feel, gradually drift closer to Russia of its own accord, recognizing that its economic, political, and security interests are best addressed through integration with Russia. At least part of this school is "re-integrationist," urging strong measures to effect a change in Russian-Ukrainian relations. Russian policy is officially integrationist, but, as will be seen below, the implementation of this stance has been pragmatic and restrained.

Ukrainian policy-makers and analysts, for their part, display two basic orientations toward Russia: nationalist and integrationist. There is also a large middle ground—itself divided into those more inclined toward a Western-oriented policy to balance Russia and those who believe in a more active partnership with Russia. These perspectives are not exactly counterparts of those in Russia, for Ukraine has more daunting problems of state-building and a more modest base upon which to build public-policy orientations. The continued weakness of the Ukrainian press, research community, and government sharply limits the number of people who actually make or influence policy toward Russia. The Ukrainian debate over relations with Russia and other national security issues is thus more inchoate and less transparent than the debate in Russia.

The Ukrainian *nationalist* orientation to Russia is perhaps the best known and most cited in Moscow itself. In embracing state-building themes, the Ukrainian government has itself at times drawn upon the nationalist heritage, but the nationalists remain mostly an opposition force. Some embrace a strong ethnic and cultural nationalism—anti-Russian by definition. More moderate nationalists simply want to break the traditional patterns between Ukraine and Moscow, yet many of them doubt whether Russia can overcome its "imperial psychology" and accept Ukrainian independence. Because of the requirements of state- and institution-building (and the strong support that nationalist and nationalist-oriented forces within Ukraine lend the state in those areas), nationalists have placed real constraints on policies toward Russia. They have clamored for a clean break

---

[43] Gennadi Zyuganov, "'Junior Partner'? No Way," *New York Times*, 1 Feb. 1996.

between Ukraine and the CIS, making it difficult to imagine any Ukrainian leadership embracing Russian integrationist plans without internal problems. Nationalists have focused on the development of a Ukrainian army as a means of self-defense. They have also argued that such an army should consist primarily of ethnic Ukrainians. Some in nationalist circles also have flirted with the notion of retaining nuclear weapons as a means of deterring Russia over the long-term. However, given their limited access to key government positions and their limited appeal to large segments of the population, nationalists have not been able to have the impact they would like on Ukrainian-Russian relations—or on Ukrainian domestic and foreign policy as a whole. Thus the nationalist agenda has only tangentially shaped Ukrainian relations with Russia.

A second Ukrainian perspective on the relationship with Russia focuses on *integration*. It is strong in the eastern regions, among old union and party functionaries and among the miners and factory workers once generously subsidized by Moscow. While the notion of attempting to accommodate Moscow to create space for Ukrainian cultural and political autonomy has deep roots in the Ukrainian national movement itself, today's accommodationists are not concerned about a prop for Ukrainian statehood, language, or culture.[44] At the fringe, few have any regard for these issues at all. In economic matters, however, this point of view has exerted real influence on Ukrainian policies. CIS and bilateral economic mechanisms have been some of the few temptations Ukrainian statesmen have actually taken seriously. In the past four years, Ukraine considered the possibility of a customs union with Russia, though it has now cooled to the idea. Russia's imposition of a 20-percent VAT on all Ukrainian imports (in October 1996) has led Ukrainian leaders to be even less enthusiastic about an open economic relationship with Russia. Ukraine agreed to the creation of a CIS inter-state economic committee but has not become a full mem-

---

[44] In the early 1900s, Ukrainian intellectuals "divided into two main orientations: the federalists, who saw the solution of the Ukrainian problem in the Russian Empire in the framework of a federation . . . ; and the independentists, who supported the idea of the national independence for the Ukraine" (Jaroslaw Pelenski, "Introduction," in *The Political and Social Ideas of Vjaceslav Lypyns'kyj*, in *Harvard Ukrainian Studies*, 9: 3-4 [Dec. 1985], pp. 238-239).

ber. President Kuchma appealed strongly to this orientation in his 1994 presidential campaign and in his first statements as president when he spoke of Ukraine as "historically part of the Eurasian economic and cultural space."[45]

But Kuchma and an overwhelming majority of other key policy-makers provide a good illustration of a broad middle ground—hardly a separate school of thought—that wants to create a stable relationship with Russia. As Kuchma has stated, "[T]here is Ukraine, and there is Russia. Both are independent states—and that is what they must continue to be. But neighbors must live together in peace and friendship. There is no other possibility."[46] In this approach, Kuchma continues a policy tradition begun by President Kravchuk before him: "We are well aware that policy with regard to Russia should be a priority for us, and the same is true of Russia's policy toward Ukraine. This is an essential condition—in light of our history, our links, and, for instance, the fact that more than 11 million Russians live in Ukraine and some 5 million Ukrainians live on Russian soil. It must also be borne in mind that we have to tackle together—on equal terms, with no senior or junior partners—huge problems that cannot be resolved otherwise."[47] The different strands of opinion within this middle ground unite on strong support for Ukrainian independence and the realization that a settlement with Russia is required; differences emerge over the mixture of closeness and distance that such a settlement entails.

These differences are real, but they do not amount to a chasm—as the press and public debate between nationalists and integrationists so frequently suggest. The differences in the middle ground are more subtle, less public, and part of an ongoing policy battle within the Ukrainian government. The high walls separating the government from the press, political analysts, and the Ukrainian public obscure much of this debate from view. Indeed, as argued in the first chapter, these walls create two, still largely separate debates—the internal and the public—on almost every important political issue. Key public figures shape

---

[45] See, for example, Kuchma's inaugural address in *Golos Ukrainy*, 21 July 1994.

[46] *Die Welt*, 3 July 1995.

[47] *FBIS Daily Report: Central Eurasia*, 12 Feb. 1992.

the public debate, but the experts and journalists outside the narrow policy-making circle are limited by a basic lack of information and interpretive framework. Often, both sides rely heavily on arguments and facts from Moscow, Washington, or Brussels, without ever fully shaping a specifically Ukrainian perspective.

THE INFLUENCE OF RUSSIAN DOMESTIC POLITICS

L ike all neighbors of a large and important state, Ukraine watches Russian domestic political trends with great care. Russian politics has a powerful influence on Ukraine, and Ukraine has internal constituencies that could be influenced by Moscow. Russian nationalist leaders in Crimea have in fact encouraged Russia to play exactly this role.

Ukrainian public statements respond to negative statements from prominent Russians with alacrity, but senior officials understand the Russian domestic requirements for bluster, and they are acutely conscious of the difference between statements by Russian parliamentarians or prominent public figures outside of government and by members of Yeltsin's inner circle.[48]

Russian domestic politics has influenced Ukraine in yet another way—one not intended by Moscow. Serious domestic crises, like the storming of the Russian Parliament in October 1993, or the invasion of Chechnya, have helped to define in stark terms the potential costs and benefits of deeper integration. Left-wing forces in Ukraine normally emphasize pocketbook issues, particularly the old system of subsidies and centralized orders that sustained much of eastern Ukraine's heavy industry and mining. But such positive—and exaggerated—images of the benefits of closer Russian-Ukrainian integration are juxtaposed in the minds of Ukrainian citizens with the

---

[48] During an interview with the author in late 1995, one senior official sketched the various factions surrounding Yeltsin and the advantages and disadvantages Ukraine might see in the rise or fall of any of them. Connections between senior Ukrainian officials and leading politicians in Moscow go back deep into Soviet times; they are the most potent of policy channels, leading to greater frankness and pragmatism than in the more publicized formal meetings or in press accounts of them.

55

potential that integration might bring entanglement in future tragedies such as Chechnya, Tajikistan, or Abkhazia. Independence has shielded a whole generation of Ukrainian youth from these conflict zones.[49]

---

[49] For evidence that, since the war in Chechnya, Ukrainians believe their state to be more stable internally, see Viktor Zamyatin, "Khorosho tam, gde nas net I nikogda ne budet," *Kommersant Daily*, 12 August 1995 and Oleksandr Stehniy, "Ukraine-Russia: Where is it Better," *Demokratychna Ukraina*, 27 Apr. 1995, p. 5; translated in *FBIS Daily Report: Central Eurasia*, 19 May 95.

CHAPTER 3
THE UKRAINIAN-RUSSIAN UNFINISHED AGENDA

Given the complex historical background of Ukrainian-Russian relations and the magnitude of coping with the great changes of the past half-decade, it is not surprising to find the two states still facing a complicated set of issues, many of which have been addressed repeatedly over the last five years.[50] A strong framework for consultations has been established to deal with this agenda, including regular meetings of the presidents, ministers, and experts. A special commission has been created—chaired by the countries' prime ministers—to address outstanding foreign policy and security issues. Foremost among these are: recognition of existing borders, integration, Ukrainian-Russian economic relations (particularly Ukraine's energy dependency), the division and basing of the Black Sea Fleet, and the future military balance between the two countries.

RECOGNITION OF BORDERS

There is no more fundamental aspect of sovereignty than international respect for existing borders. Until signature and ratification of the Friendship Treaty between the two countries removes existing ambiguities, Russian legal recognition of Ukrainian borders is conditional. The Russian government has distanced itself from overt questioning of the existing territorial divisions by prominent politicians, Duma resolutions, or even (in 1992) by the then vice president. But it has not formally agreed to unconditional recognition of Ukraine's existing borders in a treaty. To date, in fact, Russian policy has sought to maintain a linkage between Ukraine's existing borders and its participation in an integrated and formal relationship with Russia.

---

[50] See, for example, the list of "ten difficult barriers" dividing Russia and Ukraine in *Izvestiya*, 15 Jan. 1993, p. 1.

The December 1991 agreement establishing the CIS contains the following provision on the territorial integrity of the member states: "The high contracting parties recognize and respect one another's territorial integrity and the inviolability of existing borders *within the commonwealth*" (emphasis added).[51] This language has its roots in an earlier agreement—that of the November 1990 Treaty on the Basic Principles of Relations between the Russian Federation of Soviet Socialist Republics and the Ukrainian SSR—which is equally conditional in its recognition: "The high contracting parties acknowledge and respect the territorial integrity of the Ukrainian SSR and the RSFSR inside the borders presently existing *within the framework of the USSR*" (emphasis added).[52] The language of the 1991 treaty, negotiated by Vladimir Lukin and Borys Tarasyuk—two prominent figures in Russian and Ukrainian foreign policy respectively—created a strong link between Russian recognition of Ukraine's borders and continued Ukrainian participation in a broader political framework with Russia. It was obviously not the preference of the Ukrainian side, but, as Tarasyuk himself has acknowledged, it was the the best language he could get.[53]

This formula was not acceptable to the Ukrainian side. In ratifying the December 1991 CIS Agreement, the Ukrainian Parliament insisted upon making major changes in the text itself. The Parliament substituted by formal reservation an article on unconditional territorial recognition before ratifying the document—a procedure that the Rada also used in November 1993 in ratifying the Strategic Arms Reduction Treaty I (START I). The reservation with regard to border recognition states: " . . . in accordance with Article 5 of the Agreement, the High Contracting Parties recognize and respect the territorial integrity of one another and the inviolability of the state borders existing between them."[54]

This method of unilateral amendment made clear Ukraine's stance on border recognition but did not alter Russia's

---

[51] *TASS*, 9 Dec. 1991.

[52] "Treaty on the Principles of Relations Between the RSFSR and the Ukrainian SSR," Article 6. Text of treaty published in *Radyanska Ukraina*, 21 Nov. 1990, p. 1.

[53] Author's interview, Sept. 1995.

[54] The text of the Ukrainian Parliament (Rada) ratification of the Minsk Agreement Establishing a Commonwealth of Independent States was published in *Golos Ukrainy*, 14 Dec. 1991.

formal position. Russian officials continued to stress that Russia recognized Ukraine's borders "within the Commonwealth." In April 1992, Foreign Minister Andrey Kozyrev provided the Supreme Soviet with the government's official interpretation of the clauses on territorial recognition contained in the December 1991 Russian–Ukrainian–Belarusian Agreement:

> as far as the Crimea is concerned, we proceed on the basis of the agreement signed in Minsk on 8 December 1991, on the formation of the CIS, which envisages mutual recognition and respect for the territorial integrity of states that are members of the CIS and the inviolability of existing frontiers within the Commonwealth framework. I would like to stress these words—within the Commonwealth framework.[55]

The Russian government has repeatedly stated that Crimea is Ukraine's internal matter. However, the Russian Parliament voted twice in 1992 to reconsider the constitutionality of the 1954 transfer of Crimea to Ukraine and passed a resolution calling for an examination of the status of Sevastopol. Lukin expressed a preference for a region-by-region referendum to determine the ultimate status of Crimea and eastern Ukraine in his correspondence with Aleksandr Solzhenitsyn, published in *Literaturnaya gazeta* in April 1992. Then Russian Vice President Rutskoy also stated during his November 1992 visit to Omsk that he believed that Crimea would eventually return to Russia.

The Russian-Ukrainian negotiations on the comprehensive Friendship Treaty have been the key forum for resolving this tension over the recognition of existing borders. On the agenda since 1992, the treaty was originally seen by both parties as a vehicle for the comprehensive settlement of a range of issues, including dual citizenship, the Black Sea Fleet, and border recognition. The treaty has been on the verge of completion ever since. This pattern suggests the fundamental rhythm of a relationship in which the leaders quickly act to lessen tension but are unable or unwilling to resolve outstanding issues. With the election of President Kuchma, both sides planned for the quick resolution of outstanding items and a formal state visit by President Yeltsin to

---

[55] *FBIS Daily Report: Central Eurasia*, 22 Apr. 1992.

Kiev in October 1994. Continued disagreements over the treaty's language on territorial recognition, dual citizenship, and the Black Sea Fleet have led to its repeated postponement. In March 1995, the parties agreed to deal with the Black Sea Fleet and dual citizenship in separate agreements. The Friendship Treaty was initialed at that time, but it has languished in acrimonious expert discussions and as of early 1997 still has not been signed.

With help from the West, both sides took a key step toward recognition of borders with the January 1994 signing of the U.S.–Russian–Ukrainian Trilateral Agreement. The Agreement helped to resolve outstanding differences on nuclear disarmament by linking Ukrainian commitments to a series of security assurances and commitments on technical and financial assistance on the part of Russia and the United States. The Agreement reaffirms the commitment of NPT depository states, including Russia, "to Ukraine, in accordance with the principles of the Helsinki Final Act, to respect the independence and sovereignty and existing borders of Ukraine." This formula for the first time removes the clause that makes territorial recognition conditional on Ukraine's continued participation in the CIS, but it is only a politically binding document, not a legal treaty— although it is agreed upon and supported by outside powers. In winning Russian political acceptance of the strongest language to date on the inviolability of Ukraine's borders, the Trilateral Agreement has helped to steer the negotiations on the Friendship Treaty in the direction of unconditional recognition.

Several factors continue to inhibit final closure on the Friendship Treaty and thus on an acceptable and legally binding formula for border recognition. The first is the political atmosphere in Russia. During the 1996 presidential election, there was little to be gained by Yeltsin or his successor from a trip to Kiev to sign a treaty that did not in some way support the prevailing notion of CIS integration. The treaty in fact would be widely seen in Russia and Ukraine as doing just the opposite: creating the basis for Russian-Ukrainian relations outside the CIS, and on a more equal footing than many Russians desire. Even since the June 1996 presidential election, there is little apparent interest in Russia in an agreement that settles issues that many in the Russian government and foreign policy circles would prefer to remain unresolved.

The issue of border recognition illustrates a key feature of Ukrainian-Russian relations: the admixture of commitment to avoid crises and reluctance to resolve key questions once and for all. Although Russia appears to pose no imminent threat to Ukraine's existing borders, the very lack of resolution of this issue is an irritant in the bilateral relationship and could well serve as a pretext for a future Russian leadership to reopen this and other questions. Europe does not need an unresolved boundary on one of its longest and most important land borders.

CIS INTEGRATION

For Russian statesmen and analysts, promoting integration on the territory of the former USSR has been a consistent strategic imperative since at least late 1992. Integration is a term that unites government and opposition, nationalists, communists, and democrats—although this consensus covers over a great deal that is uncertain and undefined. To the nationalist and communist extremes, it means the restoration of old central economic and political ties. To others, it means a process of economic cooperation designed to address the void left by the fall of the Soviet Union and the resulting weak national economies. Policy analysts primarily interested in foreign policy and security issues see integration as responding to the problems of a currently weak zone of states and instability on Russia's border with a political and security structure shaped by Russian interests. A wide variety of opinion also exists on how integration might come to be—whether through a process of "economic interaction and inter-penetration" that respects the sovereignty of the new states, or through overt coercion, or by the failure of some of the new states to make it on their own.

Whatever "integration" means, Russian advocates intend it to solidify Russia's place on the territory of the former USSR and, by so doing, to become a strong base for restoring Russia as a great power beyond this region. Russia has been the initiator of various CIS and bilateral arrangements, such as customs or currency unions and the Tashkent Collective Security Treaty—all designed to deepen integration on the territory of the former USSR. Russian statesmen have cheered the process. President Yeltsin has maintained that there is "virtually in all CIS countries today . . . a growing desire for closer cooperation and a genuine rather than a merely declared integration."[56] Foreign Minister Primakov has called integration "the main trend in the development of our countries"[57]; he has stressed the "objective basis" for integration and has chided the West for its "primitive" view and suspicion of the process. To underscore the priority of integration and ties with Russia's new neighbors, Primakov's first trip as Foreign Minister was an extended tour of the CIS countries, including Ukraine.

For Russia, Ukraine is the key test of the direction and viability of this policy. Ukraine's participation is crucial to defining whether the CIS can meaningfully unite the key states of the former USSR. In January 1996, President Yeltsin offered eloquent testimony to this fact when he was asked by journalists which elements of a long-term integration strategy can be implemented in 1996:

> To all appearances, this will proceed not by elements, but by states. That is, today three states are already—in practice, we already have all the agreed-upon documents. These are Russia, Byelorussia [sic], and Kazakhstan. That is, we have one legal framework, the same regulations, and so on, and there are no customs borders or customs duties in bilateral trade. In short, there is a multitude of such elements which are leading up to total integration. Three more states are willing to join in that integration on the basis of appropriate documents—Uzbekistan, Tajikistan and Kyrgyzstan—three states. But when we discussed that with Ukraine . . . so far, Ukraine does not want to join integration, it does not want it, although I tried to convince them, I tried hard to convince them to agree to integration. The integration of Russia and Ukraine means the salvation of both states from the problems confronting us today. And they have no fewer problems than we do.[58]

From the Russian point of view, Ukraine adds a strong Slavic and European flavor to the CIS. It restores a European element to

---

[56] "Remarks of President Boris Yeltsin at the 49th General Assembly," 26 Sept. 1994, *Federal News Service Transcript.*

[57] "Remarks by Foreign Minister Yevgeny Primakov at the Duma Committee for International Affairs," 8 Feb. 1996, *Federal News Service Transcript.*

[58] Boris Yeltsin, "Press Conference Regarding the Results of the CIS Summit in Moscow," 19 Jan. 1996, *Federal News Service Transcript.*

what could develop into a lopsidedly "Eurasian" organization. Over time, Ukraine could become a considerable military asset to a community that already has enough members that cannot defend themselves or are a source of regional instability. Ukrainian participation would also add needed international legitimacy to Russia's integrationist policies. An integrated community without Ukraine is a serious rebuff to Russia's declared strategic interests on the territory of the former USSR and to the long-term viability of this community as a whole.

But Ukraine does not only represent a prize to be won or an opponent to be overcome, as many Russians believe. Ukrainian statesmen have defined an alternative vision of integration and cooperation in the region that is much friendlier to sovereignty and more open to the world at large than has been the case with Russian proposals. In the words of one senior Foreign Ministry official, Ukraine's view is not aimed at obtaining a "civilized divorce" and thus a permanent separation from Russia and other former Soviet republics but rather at building "normal, equal relations with Russia and all the new countries."[59] Ukraine has carved out a special status for itself within the CIS, resisting charters and other mechanisms that would transform the CIS into a supranational organization. It has placed special emphasis on economic matters, stoutly resisting all but the narrowest CIS security initiatives.[60] In Ukraine's view, all integrationist plans must be tested against the standard of national sovereignty and equality of rights for all participants.

Russia and Ukraine have differed from the very beginning on the extent and purpose of integration, and particularly over the role of the CIS. In part, this fundamental disagreement is the result of necessity more than strategy—with Ukraine placing a high price on building a state of its own at a time when Russia underscored the need for the new states to form a collective mechanism for political, economic, and security policy. Early debates formed around whether the CIS had a long-term future or served only as a convenient way out of the USSR. The former

---

[59] Author's interview, Feb. 1996.

[60] An interesting exception is Ukraine's agreement to maintain a common air defense—although only modest progress has been made in implementing this CIS agreement.

chairman of the Ukrainian Parliamentary Commission on International Affairs referred to the CIS as "a bridge . . . over the chaos," not something designed to last for centuries.[61]

Over time, a clear strategic difference has emerged between the policies of Russia and Ukraine. The Ukrainian elite has developed its own view of cooperation, even integration, providing a strong and consistent thread in Ukrainian policy and continuing under President Kuchma despite fears that he would lean too far in Russia's direction. In 1992-93, this view animated the struggle over a CIS Charter—a document Russia backed but Ukraine opposed.[62] It defined Ukraine's ultimate caution on a customs union with Russia in 1993 and Kuchma's qualified embrace of the CIS Interstate Economic Committee in late 1994. It continues to limit Ukraine's military engagement with the CIS. Indeed, this alternative strategic view of integration is not Ukraine's alone. It has resonance in other CIS successor states, particularly Uzbekistan.[63] The strategic difference between the Ukrainian and the Russian perspectives on this issue is illustrated by two documents: on the one hand, President Yeltsin's September 1995 decree defining Russia's CIS policy; on the other, the internal memorandum of Ukrainian Foreign Minister Hennady Udovenko that appeared in the newspaper *Nezavisimost*.[64]

Yeltsin's decree is entitled, "On Affirming the Strategic Course of the Russian Federation with the Member States of the Commonwealth of Independent States." The opening section states that Russia's relations with the states of the CIS are "an important factor for including Russia in world political and economic structures." The document embodies a strong Russian

---

[61] *Washington Post*, 16 Dec. 1991.

[62] On the CIS Charter, see Roman Solchanyk, "Ukraine and the CIS: A Troubled Relationship," *RFE-RL Research Report*, 2:7 (12 Feb. 1993), pp. 23-27.

[63] Fred Starr, "Making Eurasia Stable," *Foreign Affairs*, 75:1 (Jan.-Feb. 1996), pp. 80-92.

[64] Yeltsin's decree was published in *Rossiyskaya gazeta*, 23 Sept. 1995, p. 4 (translated in *FBIS Daily Report: Central Eurasia*, 28 Sept. 1995). Udovenko's memorandum was leaked to *Nezavisimost*, 5 Oct. 1995. Udovenko confirmed the authenticity of the document when he expressed "his profound regret that this letter was published at all. It is, in principle, an internal document that was not intended for publication." (Interview with Udovenko in *Mlada fronta dnes*, 9 Oct. 1995—translated *in FBIS Daily Report: Central Eurasia*, 24 Oct. 1995).

belief that integration within the CIS is a basis for Russia's reconstitution as a great power, not a distraction or a resource drain. The decree affirms the priority of Russia's relationship with the states of the CIS precisely because "on the territory of the CIS all our main vital interests are concentrated." Cooperation within the CIS framework has a restraining effect on centrifugal tendencies within Russia itself. Though there must be mutual compromises, CIS policy is ruled by the principle of "not doing harm to Russia's interests." Russian policy must concern itself with the political, economic, military, and humanitarian stability of these new states. It must encourage them to conduct policies that are friendly to Russia. It must strengthen Russia "in the capacity of the leading force for forming a new system of interstate [*mezhgosudarstvennye*] political and economic relations on the territory of the former USSR." It must expand and strengthen integrationist processes in the CIS.

After this opening discussion, the decree turns to specific areas of policy guidance, ranging from economic and security policy to the mechanism for internal policy-making in Russia. In the economic sphere, cooperation "within the framework of the Economic Union and bilaterally" is the fundamental precondition for resolving "the whole complex of questions [touching upon] the mutual relations of the member states of the CIS." The decree advocates the step-by-step expansion of the customs union and a payments union to regularize debt settlement. Although economic integration is not the only basis for relations, how partners relate to this model "will be an important factor defining the scale of economic, political, and military support from Russia."

On defense and security issues, the decree seeks "to stimulate intentions of the CIS state parties to unite in a defense alliance." It urges efforts to make already agreed cooperation in the military infrastructure more effective and to encourage Russian military bases "in cases where there is mutual interest." A key goal is obtaining from the CIS member states "the implementation of the obligation to refrain from participating in alliances and blocs directed against any of the other CIS members." Great emphasis is laid upon a common approach to the security of CIS state borders, particularly securing the legal basis for deploying Russian guards on the "outward perimeter" of the

CIS. The persistent Russian desire is to create a legal and political basis for regarding boundaries between CIS states a separate category of international boundaries—a policy Ukraine rejects.[65] As for peacekeeping and the regulation of conflicts on the territory of the CIS, the decree advocates cooperation with the United Nations and the Organization on Security and Cooperation in Europe (OSCE), but such cooperation must proceed with "understanding from their side that this region is first of all a zone of Russian interests."

With regard to human rights and humanitarian cooperation, the decree articulates a set of principles and policies designed to secure the predominant place of Russian media in the former USSR and keep Russia at the center of training for the "national cadres" of the new states. Russia strives to be "the main educational center" on the territory of the former USSR. Russia will provide cooperative programs to a CIS member state in financial, economic, military, and political areas "in direct relation to the real position [of this state] on the matter of the observance of the rights and interests of Russians [*Rossiyane*] living on its territory."

The decree represents an authoritative statement of Russian policy, although Russia's own resource constraints and its fragmented mechanism for making and carrying out foreign policy frustrate putting such policies into action. Indeed, the decree also can be read as an indicator of the level of anxiety that Russia feels about the lack of interest in integration in the former USSR in the absence of a strong and concerted push from Russia. The decree is an important indicator of the Russian leadership's preferences and goals for the CIS and its member states. It would not take a great deal of textual analysis to show that the Russians see the CIS very much as a mechanism shaped by and responding to Russian interests and power.

An internal Ukrainian policy memorandum analyzing President Yeltsin's decree—prepared for President Kuchma by Foreign Minister Udovenko and leaked to the Kiev newspaper *Nezavisimost*—reveals a Ukrainian policy that is far more than

---

[65] See, for example, the report in *OMRI Daily Digest*, 8 Jan. 1996, that Deputy Foreign Minister Konstantyn Hryshchenko said Ukraine finds it "inadmissible" to divide its borders into "internal" and "external" ones.

simply anti-CIS or anti-Russian. Its criticisms of the Russian decree are based on an alternative and sophisticated understanding of bilateral cooperation, integration, and the CIS.

Udovenko begins with an extended critique of the Russian position for its intolerance of state sovereignty. The policies outlined in the Russian president's decree suggest a pattern of interference in the internal affairs of CIS member states. Russia will stand as the arbiter of conflicts or the source of information, and it aspires to educate the next generation of leaders in the CIS. "Political and economic stability in CIS countries," Udovenko writes, "in general is valued by Russia only in cases when they follow friendly policies to Russia." The Russian concept of a commonwealth is not in keeping with that of the international community at large, which is based on the "equality of all partners." Russia seeks "domination in the region," according to Udovenko, not a commonwealth. Integration along these lines "means the watering down of the sovereignty of the CIS states."

Ukraine has an alternative view of the CIS. "[T]he CIS has a future," Udovenko writes, "and must exclusively serve to safeguard the national interests of all participating states." There is thus no need for the CIS to become a suprastate structure. Ukraine wants to maintain its neutral status and to avoid entanglement in the CIS Collective Security Treaty. Ukraine's orientation toward a model of "European unity" that is incompatible with the reemergence of blocs—its preference for the larger integrative trends in the world rather than for an exclusive focus on integration within the region—sharply differentiates its view from Russia's.

As President Kuchma reiterated during his February 1996 visit to Washington, "The question is not one of Ukraine not wanting to integrate. We have but one desire: to be open to the same prospects and processes of integration now occurring on the European continent and in the broader transatlantic space."[66] The Ukrainians, to put it simply, prefer a chance to be a part, even if a limited part, of the economically dynamic and politically open integration processes of the West. Ukraine may

---

[66] Leonid Kuchma, "Demokratychna Ukraina yak vazhlyvyi chynyk stabil'nosti u tsnetral'no skhidnii evropi" [Democratic Ukraine as an Important Factor in the Stability of Central Europe], *Remarks of the President of Ukraine, Leonid Kuchma, at Freedom House*, Washington, D.C., 21 Feb. 1996.

not be able to realize this ambition, but its leaders believe that this goal will have no chance at all if they join a closed, Russia-oriented and Russia-dominated commonwealth.

The remainder of Foreign Minister Udovenko's memo deals with the possible consequences of the implementation of Russia's strategy for a fragile Ukrainian economy. Udovenko is concerned that Russia might try to use economic levers, such as Ukraine's debt, or its dependence on the Russian market, to extract a series of concessions—particularly to effect the transfer of control over key Ukrainian economic assets and infrastructure to Russia. Udovenko provides examples, particularly of the pipeline and gas storage facilities, where the Russian Federation has made claims.

The memo does not, however, distinguish between Russian state policy and various Russian companies and industrial groups seeking a hold in the Ukrainian economy. The relationship between various Russian economic actors and the state is an important and still insufficiently examined aspect of emerging Russian foreign policy. Individual companies and economic groups are not simply tools of Russian state interests. Sometimes, the interests of these groups and the state overlap. However, there is increasing evidence, particularly in the energy sector, of these interests pursuing the maximization of their profits and influence regardless of Russian state policy.

Udovenko recommends that specific "sensitive places" in the Ukrainian economy be identified and protected from Russian encroachment. In addition, he argues that the Ukrainian government needs to understand "the farthest allowable index of economic dependence" and to work out a program to bring the actual state of the Ukrainian economy in line with this index. More work must be done to identify those sectors of the economy inextricably linked to Russia and thus most vulnerable to Russian pressure. Finally, Ukrainian diplomacy has to commence "active work with states whose views on the CIS are close to the Ukrainian one."

Ukraine's alternative strategy on integration is a combination of broad strategic vision and the constraints imposed on a geopolitically divided polity. Ukraine from the beginning could be neither fully *in* nor fully *out* of the CIS. Yet over time, Ukraine has made a virtue of this necessity. It has fashioned an intellectually respectable alternative to Russia's view of integration—one that resembles notions of economic and political intergration in the West. Ukraine's approach gives more attention than Russia's to ensuring that CIS structures remain open to integrative structures in the West.

Ukraine is not strong enough to impose its view of the future of the CIS on an unwilling Russia. It can only resist pressures to succumb to a Russian version of the commonwealth. In this Ukraine has been quite successful, for Russia is now confronted with a choice between "deepening" or "broadening" the CIS. Russia must either deepen its hold on the most willing states, such as Belarus, and thus permanently divide and weaken the CIS as a structure covering the whole of the former USSR, or it must follow a path toward cooperation very much like that sketched out by Ukraine and also favored by other CIS states.

ENERGY AND ECONOMIC TIES

Ukraine's alternative vision of cooperation deserves consideration for a further reason: there really is no way to return to a Eurasian market, political system, or security structure that rests on Russia alone. Russia is not strong enough to fulfill this role, even if its neighbors wanted it to do so. Moreover, it is questionable whether Russia could undertake such a burden and still carry through its own economic and political transformation. If Russian history is any guide, imperial or even post-imperial missions of this sort have a way of distorting reform at home. The disintegrative, regional, and local forces that brought down the USSR are hardly spent. They are reshaping the former Soviet Union in ways that make integration as a general proposition unlikely—at least on Russian terms. Where integration appears possible on Russian terms, one finds a community of states that will have trouble genuinely sharing the burdens of alliance, cooperating with one another as equals, or remaining equal partners with Russia. If the CIS is to be an effective community, it has to be made compatible with the sovereignty and interests of Ukraine and the other newly independent states.

Ukraine's debt and energy problems are acute and lack easy solutions, particularly given the country's lack of progress in energy conservation. Moreover, Western attention in the energy sphere has focused almost exclusively on shutting down the nuclear reactor at Chernobyl. Nuclear energy provides approximately 40 percent of Ukraine's electricity. While alternative energy sources are being explored, for the foreseeable future, Ukraine must rely on Russian oil and Russian and Turkmen gas—thereby increasing its indebtedness to Russia and Turkmenistan, remaining vulnerable to Russian pressure, and alienating European assistance.

As Foreign Minister Udovenko's memorandum highlights, Russian negotiators have sought to swap Ukrainian debt for critical assets, such as control over the pipeline that passes through Ukraine, or a controlling interest in the refineries at Kremenchug, Lisichansk, and other sites.[67] However, a government-to-government deal of this sort hardly makes the basic problem any easier to resolve, and Ukraine has resisted such a debt-equity swap. The gas pipeline that runs through Ukraine represents a substantial asset—one Ukraine has used to balance rising energy indebtedness to Russia by raising pipeline transit fees. In the absence of a coherent energy policy, the problems in this sector could over time grow to exert a decisive pressure on other aspects of Ukrainian politics, economics, and foreign policy.

The interesting question is why Russia, with its obvious potential for influencing Ukrainian economic life, has to date been so ineffective in wielding it. Several factors have made it difficult for Russia to use the leverage that most outside observers assume it has. The first is Russia's inability to handle the consequences of applying a draconian shutdown of Ukrainian energy supplies. Russia has European customers on the other side of the pipeline who would not tolerate a long-term break in service. Moreover, a Ukraine in economic chaos is not a burden Russia could bear. A second reason is the existence of profiteers on both sides, inside and outside government, who have benefited from the energy transfer. Large amounts of money have been generated by selling subsidized oil at world market prices—even when the Russian government received no payment and the Ukrainian government piled up debt. Ukraine is now paying its current account and handling a large part of its

---

[67] For a Russian view of the Ukrainian energy complex, see A. N. Loginov, "Problemy toplivno-energeticheskogo kompleksa Ukrainy," *Ukraina: Vektor peremen*, Moscow: RISI, 1994, pp. 27-41.

energy transactions through several private holding companies established by the government, but the profit motive remains. Ukraine still receives energy at slightly below world market prices. In the past, when the price was substantially below world market levels, the profits from such sales were enough to grease pockets in Kiev, Moscow, and a number of places in between. Such possibilities will continue to be exploited for sometime to come, though they are limited by genuine reform on both sides of the border.

Finally and perhaps most important, Russia is by no means a unitary economic actor. Its energy companies want profits, markets, and infrastructure. The government wants geopolitical leverage over Ukraine. In some instances, particularly on schemes that would swap assets for debt, the companies and the government see eye to eye. But on other issues, particularly on turning off the spigot to increase geopolitical leverage, the two are unlikely to agree. Companies like Lukoil and Gazprom want to maximize profits and market share. They are successfully doing this on their own and do not need to make themselves the tools of a weak Russian foreign policy. Gazprom and other large energy suppliers cannot be compelled to play a subordinate role in Russian energy and CIS policy. It is not in Gazprom's interest to cease delivery of gas to Ukraine for Russian political purposes: they operate more and more on a profit, not political, basis. The Russian government has less and less leverage over them and thus no real power to conduct a unified policy of economic boycotts or sanctions. Yet these companies are seeking to expand their presence in the Ukrainian market and will almost certainly create a substantial Russian presence there over time. The long-term question for Ukraine is whether this presence could in the future be made to serve the interests of a revived Russian state, or whether Ukrainian economic reform will attract sufficient outside investment from other sources to offset Russian economic leverage.

Thus, beyond the obvious internal imperatives, economic reform has a strategic significance for Ukraine. An economically viable Ukraine would be in a position to have a more normal consumer-producer relationship with Russia.

Economic reform is also the beginning of a prudent energy policy. Reform would remove remaining energy subsidies and eliminate special deals and other arrangements that prevent the forces of the market from working in the energy sector. If Ukraine got used to paying world market prices, it would be less vulnerable. Ukraine must also quicken the pace toward a full-blown energy policy, upgrading indigenous sources of energy and electrical power and forcing its industries to become more energy-efficient. Without real progress in this area, Ukraine will remain vulnerable to future energy pressure from Russia.

Energy may be Ukraine's Achilles' heel, but problems have crept into the overall Russian-Ukrainian economic relationship as well. In October 1996, Russia imposed a 20 percent VAT on Ukrainian imports and a strict quota on Ukrainian sugar, leaving both countries on the brink of a trade war. The two nations are one another's largest trading partners, though the greatest effect would fall on Ukraine. Russian products accounted for over 37 percent of total imports in the first half of 1996.[68] The Russian side claims that Ukrainian goods are being dumped on the Russian market. Ukraine sees Russian policies as part of a growing pattern of economic intimidation. This issue, like so many on the Russian-Ukrainian agenda, is unlikely to be resolved without pressure from the outside. The most promising candidates for applying such pressure are the international financial institutions, particularly the IMF, which played a key role in the 1995 bilateral debt rescheduling.

THE BLACK SEA FLEET

The Black Sea Fleet has been a matter of controversy since 1992.[69] In the aftermath of the fall of the Soviet Union, Russia believed the Fleet would remain a joint strategic asset of the CIS. Ukraine, however, did not regard the Fleet as a strategic asset but as a national one, and it claimed the entire Fleet for itself. Russia quickly followed suit, which led to a serious escalation of tensions as both sides issued claims and counterclaims that were only resolved when they agreed to divide the Fleet's assets and basing rights in August 1992. This 1992 agreement,

---

[68] *The Financial Times*, 10 Sept. 1996.
[69] This discussion is adapted and updated from the author's article, "U.S. National Interests in Crimea," in *Crimea: Dynamics, Challenges and Prospects*, ed. Maria Drohobycky, (Lanham, MD: Rowan and Littlefield, 1995), pp. 195-209.

reconfirmed on several occasions, has been the basis for long and contentious negotiations between Russia and Ukraine on establishing the formal division of the Fleet and its property and the basing arrangements for both its Russian and Ukrainian components. These negotiations continue at the expert level and are the subject of ministerial meetings and summits. The two sides regularly announce breakthroughs, most recently in October 1996, but these unravel within days after their announcement. Meanwhile, the Fleet has not remained static. Russia has de facto control over the bulk of its assets, with the fledgling Ukrainian navy attempting to establish its presence on the peninsula. There have been frequent incidents involving the sailors of the two navies. One of these, in May 1994, involved a Russian seizure of a scientific research ship from a port on the Ukrainian mainland. A chase ensued that led to the firing of tracer bullets. As long as the Fleet remains an issue, its sailors and associated military units represent a potential source of conflict on the volatile Crimean peninsula.

Composed of aging vessels, port, and support facilities (chiefly in Sevastopol), the Black Sea Fleet is less important as a military asset than as a signal of the state of Ukrainian-Russian relations, the viability of Ukrainian sovereignty over Crimea, and Russia's long-term presence and influence on the Black Sea. Two basic issues shape the bilateral negotiations: the numerical division of the Fleet and its assets, and Russian basing rights at Sevastopol.

The division of the Fleet is basically settled, lacking only the signature and ratification of a final treaty. A formula for the division of the Fleet that meets the requirements and financial abilities of both sides was agreed in early 1994. Ukraine is to receive approximately 160 of the more than 800 ships counted as part of the Fleet. This deal was confirmed in June 1995, when the Ukrainian and Russian presidents met at Sochi, and again in October 1996. Although the exact details of the negotiation process will not be known until the agreement is completed, the two sides appear to have agreed on a roughly 80-20 split between Ukraine and Russia respectively, with Moscow "purchasing" the remainder of Ukraine's 50 percent entitlement as debt forgiveness. The outcome gives Russia the preponderance of the Fleet that it sought from the beginning but allows the

Ukrainian side both to claim that it stuck to its principle of a 50-50 split and to receive financial benefit from surrendering 30 percent of a decaying Fleet it could not maintain and did not need in the first place.

The numbers were probably never that crucial. Ukraine cannot support a large blue-water navy—but neither can Russia. The current economic pressure, coupled with honest assessments of naval requirements in the region, ought to reduce the overall number of ships of both navies over time. This reduction is likely to be crucial for the lessening of tensions between the two countries and for the long-term diversification of the Crimean economy.

In the past several decades, the Black Sea Fleet—despite its proud history—has been a waning naval force incapable of performing the role Soviet defense planners assigned it in the Mediterranean against the U.S. Sixth Fleet and other NATO assets. With the disappearance of Soviet strategic requirements along with the Soviet Union itself, and with the collapse of the Russian and Ukrainian economies, the military effectiveness of the Black Sea Fleet is of little consequence to NATO. The real military tasks it must perform in small-scale regional conflicts and coastal defense do not warrant maintenance of the current Fleet and support facilities.

However, their maintenance is important to the local population, which is economically dependent upon the Fleet. As former Crimean Prime Minister Saburov has pointed out, the Fleet and other Crimean military installations are an economic and political issue, as they support the surrounding civilian population, including a large group of military retirees. This link will not be easily broken, particularly at a time when the peninsula faces increasing economic hardship.[70] However, a long-term economic development plan in Crimea, coupled with the reduction of the Fleet to the level of military requirements, could play a positive role in reducing the potential for Russian-Ukrainian tensions.

The second issue—the basing of the newly divided Fleet—has been the main item of contention for years. Central to the issue is the status of Sevastopol and the larger question of the

---

[70] Yevgeni Saburov, "The Socioeconomic Situation in Ukraine," in *Crimea: Dynamics, Challenges and Prospects*, op. cit., pp. 15-37.

long-term Russian military presence in Crimea. A near-term Russian withdrawal from Crimea—as advocated by former Ukrainian Defense Minister Morozov—is not feasible, both because of Russian fiscal constraints and the sentiments of the local Crimean population.[71] Both sides are thus negotiating the conditions under which a Russian Fleet will remain. Russian proposals and press commentary stress the need for a permanent Russian presence. The Russians have proposed a variety of long-term leasing arrangements. They obtained just such a deal in negotiations with Kazakhstan over the space launch facility at Baykonur, which obviously provides for the Russian side both a model and a precedent for talks with Ukraine. Under the Baykonur agreement, Russia provides compensation (cash and debt relief) to Kazakhstan in exchange for a long-term lease (20 years, with a 10-year renewal); the leased facility and surrounding city is considered sovereign Russian territory.

Ukraine cannot accept such an arrangement. For Ukraine, the central issue is the preservation of its sovereignty over all of Crimea. In its current political and economic state, Ukraine knows it cannot make the Russians leave, but it also cannot accept a deal that appears to cede de facto sovereignty over Sevastopol to Russia. Ukrainian negotiators know they must have a deal that limits the length of Russian presence (even if it is renewed several times) and provides real compensation, unambiguous Ukrainian sovereignty over the port and city of Sevastopol, and continued access to Crimean facilities for the Ukrainian navy. Russian nationalist politicians in Crimea—and perhaps throughout eastern Ukraine—will be watching this aspect of the agreement closely for signs that Kiev's hold over heavily Russified areas is weakening or Russia's interest in intervening in Ukrainian affairs is growing.

The current political environment in Russia is hardly propitious for a settlement. In February 1996, the Russian Duma voted overwhelmingly (315-1) to halt the partition of the Fleet.[72]

---

[71] Morozov's 1994 memoirs, which he circulated as campaign literature during his unsuccessful bid for a seat in the Rada in March 1994, make plain his differences with Kravchuk, Kuchma, and then Deputy Prime Minister Valerii Shmarov over Russian basing of the Black Sea Fleet. See *Ukrainska hazeta*, Vols. 1-4, 1994.

[72] *The Jamestown Foundation Monitor*, 16 Feb. 1996; and *OMRI Daily Digest*, 24 Oct. 1996.

The Duma voted on a similar resolution in October—again with near unanimity in favor of halting partition. In postponing his scheduled state visit to Ukraine in April 1996, President Yeltsin cited the lack of progress on the Black Sea Fleet as a factor. Prime Minister Viktor Chernomyrdin repeated Yeltsin's actions in November 1996, also pointing to the lack of resolution on the Black Sea Fleet as the main factor. Yet time is working against the Fleet as a military asset. Even if more resources are found for the Russian military, the needs of the Fleet are so great and have such a low priority that it will be difficult to do more than soften the gradual but inevitable decline of the current Black Sea Fleet and its facilities. This fact remains Ukraine's long-term leverage in the negotiations for an eventual settlement. The Ukrainian side is also reluctant to force the pace and thus to add an additional element of economic strain on an already fragile Crimea.

This issue remains a classic example of the two sides' ability to maintain enough pragmatism at key moments to avoid a breakdown, yet failing to arrive at a resolution of key issues. For both Ukraine and Russia, settlement would send strong political signals that neither can control. Even though both sides have agreed to separate this issue from the negotiation of a friendship treaty, it will remain a source of friction for some time to come.

THE RUSSIAN-UKRAINIAN MILITARY BALANCE

The future shape of the Ukrainian and Russian militaries is also an undeveloped item on the bilateral agenda that is likely to emerge in the coming decade. At present, the weakness and internal chaos of both militaries limit their importance to the bilateral relationship. Both are suffering a prolonged period of military weakness, which by no means rules out violence as an instrument of policy. It does, however, make it harder for this set of leaders to use military power in ordinary times as a regular lever of influence in the relationship. It makes a premeditated use or threat of use of such force less likely even as it increases the vulnerability of both sides to outbreaks of violence among non-state actors. The weakness of state-controlled forces, whether military or internal security, gives room for maneuver to extremist ethnic Russian, Crimean Tatar, or Ukrainian nationalist organizations, some of which have paramilitary units—or even to units of the Black Sea Fleet, which could see their attachment to local commanders and the local population as superseding that to naval and civilian authorities in Moscow.

The Russian military decline has been precipitous, consistent, and so far without reversal.[73] President Yeltsin, Defense Minister Igor Rodionov, and other senior officials have embraced the goal of modernization of the current military into smaller, more technologically sophisticated forces by 2010. However, to date, the leadership has yet to take any major steps toward reform.

Despite their size and major deployments within the European region, Russian conventional forces are not configured for offensive action. Their uneven distribution throughout the Russian Federation is the result of the pullout from Central Europe of over 700,000 military personnel and 45,000 pieces of equipment[74]—an immense undertaking accomplished with great professionalism. Russia was not prepared for their redeployment, which began even before there was an independent Russia. Until 1991, when the Kiev Military District became foreign soil, the Soviet military looked to it as a new second echelon and thus proper home for much of the returning equipment. Moreover, the withdrawal from Central Europe created force pockets and bottlenecks; in Kaliningrad, for example, it concentrated tanks and other equipment. Indeed, the greatest immediate concern about these force pockets is not that they reflect Moscow's strategy, but that they might, like the 14th Army in Moldova, not remain entirely within Moscow's control.

Resource constraints make military reform a gargantuan undertaking. The Navy must consolidate under greatly constricted funding, which is likely to doom both the Baltic and Black Sea Fleets to continued erosion and perhaps extinction.[75] As for

---

[73] This discussion of Russian military reconstitution is adapted from the author's article, "Poland: Bulwark or Bridge?," *Foreign Policy*, 102 (Spring 1996), pp. 66-82; and from his paper, *The Impact of the New Borderlands on the Russian Military*, Occasional Paper No. 9 (Cambridge, MA: American Academy of Arts and Sciences, Aug. 1995).

[74] "Press Conference with Defense Minister Pavel Grachev (Armed Forces General Headquarters), 6 May 1995, *Federal News Service Transcripts*.

[75] During the 1996 presidential campaign, Yeltsin made a special point of visiting the Baltic Fleet in Kaliningrad and promising to sustain and improve it. The basic trend lines, however—unless Yeltsin's pledge turns out to be more than a campaign promise—are for continued erosion of these smaller fleets and the concentration of remaining naval forces in the Northern and Pacific Fleets.

ground forces, these same constraints—with or without the limits imposed by the Treaty on Conventional Forces in Europe (CFE)—leave room for no more than 30 divisions west of the Urals. Both former National Security Advisor Aleksandr Lebed and General Rodionov have spoken of Russia's inability to sustain even this many divisions, thus raising the question of whether Russia would be able to station as many as 20-30 divisions in regions of relevance to Ukraine.[76] In any event, only a fraction, say 5-10 divisions, will be at a high state of readiness. The USSR in the late 1970s and 1980s stationed more divisions than this—at a higher state of readiness—in what is now Belarus, the Baltic states, and western Ukraine. Even if the Russians decide to renounce the CFE Treaty, and if the upper limit on Russian military equipment and personnel west of the Urals disappears, there will continue to be near-term constraints on resources to build, equip, deploy, and train an effective army, navy, and air force.

Moreover, the military must respond to contingencies elsewhere in the region, particularly in the Caucasus, and any reinforcement must now come from beyond the Urals. Much of the conventional, air, and air-defense infrastructure is now in the wrong place or even outside Russian control. A new infrastructure, reflecting Russia's new security environment, must be reconstituted through a mixture of diplomatic arrangements with neighbors and new construction. At present, the lack of this structure is an advantage in Ukrainian-Russian relations. The border remains unfortified. Neither side is constructing a military infrastructure that threatens the other or increases military capabilities along or near the common border.

Even if Yeltsin had not won the 1996 elections and a nationalist or national-communist administration had come to power, serious resource constraints would continue to stand in the way of a reconstitution of anything like the old Russian or Soviet military threat in the region. A determined leadership could devote increased resources to the military, but in the near term, that military must provide basic services, such as housing, wages, health care, and food where there are currently extreme shortages. Some

---

[76] See, for example, General Lebed's interview in *Nezavisimaya gazeta*, 5 July 1996, pp. 1-2; and General Rodionov's interview in *Moskovskie Novosti*, 11-18 August 1996, No. 32, p. 7.

experts have even warned that the collapse of this support system is having serious consequences for the integrity of the army.[77] A leader bent on restoring Russian military glory would have to devote a great deal of treasure to these basic building-blocks of morale. In addition, the maintenance of a Russian nuclear force will remain the highest priority, particularly given the decline of Russian conventional military power. Some Russian military analysts have even urged a radical rethinking of the utility of tactical nuclear weapons, though their redeployment would require a robust supporting conventional structure. The Russians are discovering what the United States and NATO knew throughout the Cold War: conventional forces are expensive. Nuclear weapons must compensate for conventional shortcomings that are likely to be enduring, and a strategy of nuclear deterrence is a cost-effective alternative. Moreover, nuclear weapons are the only aspect of the current defense posture that grants Russia status as a major power. Russia's first inclination is to preserve these weapons, though probably at much lower levels. It certainly cannot contemplate a major conventional build-up that would drain resources from maintaining a nuclear deterrent.

The current force structure is living off the Soviet military legacy in basic equipment and weapons systems. This Soviet largesse will provide the basis for the maintenance of a much smaller force for perhaps the next five to ten years. After that, new equipment will have to come on line to sustain even the reduced force structure currently envisioned. Russia is producing few tanks and fighter aircraft. Reconstitution will require large amounts of money to re-start military production. Arms sales are widely seen in Russian quarters as providing a transitional basis for supporting indigenous production capabilities, but they seem unlikely to be sufficiently lucrative to pay for the kind of military research and production levels necessary to meet Russia's needs in the next decade and beyond. Finally, existing and future military resources must also cover the cost of fighting ongoing or future conflicts in Chechnya, Tajikistan, Abkhazia, or elsewhere. There are also a number of important commitments, including the building of new bases and the restoration of inte-

---

[77] Colonel Yu. Deryugin, "Trevozhnye tendentsii v rossiyskoy armii," *Nezavisimaya gazeta*, 24 Aug. 1994.

grated air defense, border, and other military systems on the territory of other CIS states. The possibility of a long-term military threat from China is also unclear—though hardly one that a prudent military planner would want to ignore in favor of rebuilding offensive capability in the west.

Ukrainian military forces are in no better shape. Although Ukraine inherited some of the best infrastructure in the former USSR, as well as over 700,000 troops, 6,000 tanks, and 1,400 combat aircraft, the task of organizing this legacy into a real national military was and is a daunting one.[78] Former Defense Minister Konstantyn Morozov told a visiting U.S. delegation in 1994 that his department had to work on "month-to-month" allocations.[79] Inflation and resource constraints made sound planning impossible. Reductions were urgently needed and have been carried out, with current personnel numbering perhaps 450,000. The reductions have been slowed, however, by the military's inability to provide adequate housing, support, and career opportunities for those officers staying in the service. The slowness of economic reform in Ukraine has also limited prospects for those leaving the service, causing many military officers to cling to their meager but predictable life. The key task of the military during this time was not so much to be ready for combat as to ensure a cadre of loyal officers. Real questions continue to be raised about the direction of military education, with tension emerging between those who, like the members of the Ukrainian Officers' Union, advocate a more ethnically Ukrainian approach to officer education, and those who argue that Ukraine must stick to a military education that embraces a diversity of ethnic backgrounds yet stresses politically rooted concepts of loyalty to the state.

Educating and sustaining a strong officer corps and providing basic support and training to officers and the enlisted alike remain core military preoccupations. Military district boundaries inherited from the Soviet Union have been redrawn, but little has been done to define the future strategy and supporting force structure of the Ukrainian military. There have

---

[78] Ustina Markus, "No Longer as Mighty," *Transition*, 28 July 1995, pp. 24-29.
[79] Author's interviews with senior U.S. and Ukrainian defense officials, May, June and October 1994.

been no substantial redeployments. There is no money to correct mal-deployments made under the old Soviet defense plans. Despite reductions in force structure and personnel, Ukraine does not have the money to pay for equipment maintenance and modernization.[80] Like Russia, Ukraine faces the problem of maintaining its force structure intact as key systems reach the end of their expected life cycle. Ukraine has important pieces of the old Soviet defense industrial complex, particularly for the production of ballistic missiles, tanks, and other armored vehicles and some kinds of aircraft or their key components. But there is no possibility that Ukraine can sustain even its reduced military through indigenous production. In the near term, support for Ukraine's main military systems requires Russian industrial assistance or a massive influx of Western equipment—both unlikely prospects. Basic military questions—such as the threats Ukraine faces, future military strategy to meet them, and the operational deployment and structure of the forces to support this strategy—remain unaddressed.

Both an advantage and a danger underlie the current constraints on the military in Russia and in Ukraine. The advantage, a short- to medium-term one, is that neither military can serve as an effective and reliable instrument of national policy. Both sides seem to understand the price that would be paid for a militarization of the relationship. Neither side can be confident it could control an ignited conflict. However, the above-noted weakness of the military and other state structures in both countries has opened up new opportunities for local and private groups to act in their stead. The longer-term danger lies in assuming that this weakness is or can be permanent. Both Moscow and Kiev must inevitably decide basic questions of military and security policy that will make their bilateral relationship and regional military balances more or less secure. It remains in the long-term interest of Moscow, Kiev, and the West that these decisions be built upon the most stable aspects of the current inheritance, particularly upon its low levels of military force and their disengagement. Both sides should seek to avoid defense decisions that reverse this trend toward stability at low levels of military power. They should

---

[80] IISS's *Military Balance 1996-1997* (p. 101) lists Ukrainian tank holdings as 4,026—a reduction of nearly 1,300. Combat air holdings have also been reduced to 789, plus 380 in storage.

avoid a militarization of the Ukrainian-Russian border. Policies to encourage just such unilateral and bilateral defense policies ought to be an important element of future Western defense and arms control policy in Europe.

CONCLUSION

Those who predicted the early shipwreck of Ukrainian-Russian relations were wrong. Despite serious internal pressures, a host of disagreements, and deep differences in outlook, both Russian and Ukrainian senior officials on both sides have regularly demonstrated a high degree of pragmatism whenever it has really mattered. The two sides have "muddled through" for over five years. Diplomatic observers are now accustomed to the cycle of hopeful announcements, disappointments, crises, and reconciliations that never quite settle the basic issues that divide these two nations.

Yet the long-term character of Ukrainian-Russian relations is unsettled and potentially unsettling for Europe. The internal distractions that prevent Russia from exerting its power are not permanent. As they disappear, basic differences over the relationship will have to be resolved. Russia desires "a fraternal Slavic compromise" and integration; Ukraine wants normal state-to-state ties. It would be dangerous to assume that the current pragmatism can endure indefinitely. A stronger, more assertive Russia would have real levers of influence over Ukraine, especially if the latter had not used its "breathing space" for sweeping political and economic reforms.

The one flashpoint in the relationship that will remain for years to come is Crimea, where profound ethnic and social tensions, economic collapse, and the presence of a declining Black Sea Fleet provide a potentially combustible mixture. Even this danger probably could be significantly reduced by the resolution of current Russian-Ukrainian differences and a Western policy that recognizes that this crucial relationship cannot be left outside its concerns.

At present, one can be thankful that both sides retain the intention to continue their sensitive balancing acts, but all parties and Europe as a whole must begin to prepare for the time when this good intention no longer will be enough.

CHAPTER 4

THE EMERGING SECURITY ENVIRONMENT OF CENTRAL AND EASTERN EUROPE

For the first time in centuries, the balance between the states of Central and Eastern Europe and outside powers has shifted in favor of the former. The states of the region have or are acquiring the capacity to shape their own destinies. Russian power has contracted, and German power has been transformed—linked to strong European and trans-Atlantic institutions. Although both Russian and Western influences will continue to matter, they are no longer supreme. Ukraine and its neighbors carry on a complex and expanding diplomatic agenda that regrettably still goes largely unnoticed in the West and is misunderstood or dismissed in Moscow. Yet Ukrainian-Polish and Ukrainian-Romanian relations already suggest patterns of cooperation and friction that could affect the region as a whole. The basic conditions that led to separatist violence in Moldova remain unresolved; this violence has already brought the intervention of Russia and remains the preoccupation of both Romania and Ukraine. Even the more familiar issues of the region's interaction with the outside world—such as the potential impact of NATO expansion or Russian-Belarusian integration—are not simply manifestations of rival outside forces imposing themselves upon the region but grow out of the different orientations of the states of the region.

A new set of intra-regional relationships and a nascent but growing capacity to manage and respond to outside forces marks Eastern and Central Europe. At the same time, however, the states of the region are developing unequally, with the division especially pronounced between those with and those without real historical experience of statehood. This creates a basic division between "haves" and "have-nots" on political, economic, and security issues—a division exacerbated by different orientations among the states of the region toward the outside world. Although most of these states look to the West for membership in economic and security institutions, only Poland, the Czech Republic, and Hungary are on the brink of NATO membership and have good but more distant prospects of membership in the European Union. At the opposite end of the spectrum, only Belarus looks East: in spring 1996, it signed a bilateral agreement on integration with Russia as well as a four-power agreement to create an even wider community with Russia and two Central Asian states, Kazakhstan and Kyrgyzstan. The rest of the states fall between. The Baltic states are unlikely to see their West-oriented ambitions fulfilled in the near term. Slovakia, professing a Western orientation, has done all it can to make itself unwelcome there. Ukraine, as we have noted, is neither East nor West but crucial to the prospects of both.

A thriving and independent Ukraine could stabilize this middle zone of states, ensuring that CIS integration will either be limited, or will take on a more open, less confrontational character. It might lower the costs and security consequences of NATO expansion, helping to preserve the low levels of conventional forces and the prevention of a new nuclear confrontation—goals that NATO-expansion advocates claim as their first priority. A foundering Ukraine, in contrast, would become a source of regional instability and international discord. Ukraine's weakness would tempt Russian intervention and place immense burdens on the states forming NATO's new front-line. Such a scenario could unfold to become a modern version of the "Eastern question" as outside powers seek to gain from Ukraine's troubles—or at least to control their consequences. Ukraine is a representative *par excellence* of the "lands between," the fate of which is likely to determine whether the security arrangements now contemplated for Europe will be effective and enduring. In light of the changing dynamics within the region and Ukraine's central role there, this chapter will explore some of the basic building-blocks of the new regional security environment, with special attention to those directly linked to Ukraine.

RELATIONS WITH OTHER STATES OF THE REGION

The contraction of Russian power and Russia's internal preoccupations have given the states of Central and Eastern Europe an unprecedented role in determining the basic structure and direction of the region. These new states represent security challenges and opportunities in their own right. They threaten one another with internal instabilities and harbor regional ambitions that could produce frictions among them. They also offer new sources of support and cooperation. Although the links between these states matter in ways that could hardly have been imagined a decade ago, they still are not sufficiently studied or understood. For Kiev, three key regional relationships stand out for their importance to its foreign policy: the deepening of ties with Poland, continuing friction with Romania, and the potential for renewed violence and outside intervention in Moldova.

UKRAINIAN-POLISH RELATIONS

From Ukraine's perspective, the most promising and important partner of these three states is Poland. While both countries have recognized the need to develop ties—and Poland has from the very beginning understood the security benefits of an independent Ukraine—the history of the relationship has been one of great initial success and good will, followed by an extended period of stalled momentum. In mid-1995, both countries realized that more effort needed to be devoted to their bilateral relations. New efforts were begun under Presidents Lech Walesa and Leonid Kuchma and have continued under the new Polish President Aleksander Kwasniewski. President Kuchma's visit to Warsaw in June 1996 represented a strong signal of continuity in Ukraine's policy toward Poland.

Two contradictory expectations surrounded the initial phase of Ukrainian-Polish relations in the period 1990-93. The first was fear of the return of historical tensions; the second, the necessity of partnership. Warsaw and Kiev made real progress toward long-term cooperation during this initial period, eliminating potential stumbling blocks over borders and forming an institutional network for cooperation at the highest levels. But

85

neither the fear of renewed tension nor real accomplishment shaped bilateral ties as strongly as the preoccupation of both capitals with the political and economic issues, which robbed Ukrainian-Polish ties of much of their momentum in 1993-95. Both countries understand the potential importance of their bilateral ties, and both face the task of building on a sound but neglected base.

It is useful to recall these contradictory expectations and the solid beginnings of the Ukrainian-Polish relationship in attempting to understand the problems and prospects for these ties today. The historical legacy of Ukrainian-Polish relations includes gradual Polish political expansion over large parts of what is now Ukraine. Much of the current Ukraine west of the Dnieper River was a part of the Polish Commonwealth. Here Polish noblemen controlled large tracts of land that Ukrainian peasants lived on, producing class tensions that in the nineteenth century became national tensions. Even in the eighteenth century, when Poland itself was partitioned, the Poles regarded the whole of this territory as an integral part of Poland. In 1918-19, Poles and Ukrainians fought each other for control of eastern Galicia. During World War II, Ukrainian and Polish groups massacred each other, attempting to enforce ethnic separation in Galicia.[81] Post–World War II border adjustments and population transfers also added to the legacy of distrust.

In the recent past, as Ukrainian independence approached, voices on both sides expressed fears that future relations would be tense. A 1992 poll showed that 38 percent of Poles believed Ukraine to be Poland's greatest threat.[82] The ability on both sides to avoid taking up where the Polish-Ukrainian relationship left off prior to the sovietization of Poland and the western Ukrainian lands represents an enormous and still undervalued accomplishment. Thus for both Kiev and Warsaw, the legacy of past Polish-Ukrainian friction has proven less powerful than the new regional dynamics.

From the first signs of internal collapse of the USSR, many

---

[81] Orest Subtelny, *Ukraine: A History* (Toronto: University of Toronto, 1988), pp. 474-475.

[82] F. Stephen Larrabee, *East European Security After the War* (Santa Monica, CA: RAND, 1993) p. 19 (note).

in Poland understood the importance of a stable, independent Ukraine as a check on the reconstitution and reach of Russian power. During the early days of U.S.–Ukrainian relations, senior Polish officials warned their U.S. counterparts not to forget the value of an independent Ukraine even if nuclear disarmament did not proceed as swiftly or smoothly as originally hoped. Some commentators even saw Warsaw and Kiev as a "new strategic axis."[83]

A cooperative impulse was strong in the early days of post-Soviet Ukrainian-Polish ties—although its source was as likely to be a wish to avoid potential conflicts as a desire to build a strategic partnership. As early as October 1990, after the declarations of sovereignty by both the Ukrainian SSR and the Russian Federation, Polish Foreign Minister Krzysztof Skubiszewski traveled to Minsk, Kiev, and Moscow to establish ties paralleling—and independent of—ties with the USSR. In December 1991, Poland was the first state to recognize Ukrainian independence. A modest Ukrainian-Polish military cooperation agreement followed in January 1992 and a friendship treaty in May. Each side renounced border claims against the other. By the end of the year, a Ukrainian-Polish Presidential Consultative Committee was in place.

From December 1992 to May 1993, there was a flurry of visits to Kiev by high-level Polish officials: Foreign Minister Skubiszewski in December, Prime Minister Hanna Suchocka in January, Defense Minister Janusz Onyszkiewicz in February, and Lech Walesa himself in May, when he made the memorable statement often quoted in both capitals: "It is impossible to imagine Europe without a democratic and independent Ukraine."[84] But this initial period of cooperation reached its inherent limits. Neither country could create a "strategic axis" from its own resources. Once the basic sources of tension had been eliminated and the foundations for long-term cooperation were in place, both sides reverted to more pressing internal political and economic matters. There was little energy left for grand foreign policy initiatives not directly related to core con-

---

[83] Ian J. Brzezinski, "Polish-Ukrainian Relations: Europe's Neglected Strategic Axis," *Survival*, 35: 3 (Autumn 1993), pp. 26-37.
[84] BBC Summary of World Broadcasts, 26 May 1993.

cerns. Both countries pushed the relationship to the back burner in favor of more urgent interests.

Economic and political reforms in the two states were not proceeding in parallel. Polish economic and political reforms were far more advanced; the Ukrainian economy, hurtling toward hyperinflation, hardly represented an opportunity for Poland. Ukrainian political stability itself was a question during 1993-94. Although President Kravchuk seemed ready for stronger ties with Poland and other European states—he even proposed a "zone of security and stability" for the states of the region in April 1993—his own position was hardly secure. With the election of President Kuchma in 1994, Poland had reason to wait and see whether Ukraine would turn toward integration with Russia. In November 1993, Poland got a new Prime Minister—Waldemar Pawlak, the leader of the Polish Peasants' Party (PSL)—who, in the words of one analyst, "thought he saw in Russia a market for Polish agriculture" and therefore was reluctant to commit to any Ukrainian initiative that would alienate Russia.[85] The Left's victory in the November 1995 presidential elections also raised questions about whether Polish policy would not accelerate the tendency to deepen Poland's ties with Russia at the expense of Ukraine.

Perhaps the most important factor in the loss of momentum was the fact that Poland's fortunes were beginning to improve in the West. In 1992, Walesa had proposed a "NATO-bis" alliance of regional states as a halfway house on what appeared the long and doubtful road to eventual NATO membership. Although this proposal died quickly, it indicated the extent to which senior Polish leaders acknowledged the need to think about alternative security structures in the absence of any realistic possibility of entering NATO. In late 1993 and early 1994, Poland saw a shift for the better in its prospects for future NATO membership. President Yeltsin appeared to endorse Polish hopes during his August 1993 visit to Warsaw, though the Russian government later spent a great deal of time and effort retracting his comment. President Clinton made NATO expansion a top priority, a

---

[85] Stephen Burant, "Poland's Eastern Policy, 1990-1995: The Limits of the Possible," *Problems of Post Communism*, 43:2 (Mar.-Apr. 1996), p. 52. Burant rightly points out, however, that Poland's coolness toward Ukraine predated the appointment of the PSL leader as Prime Minister.

matter of "when, not if" during his January 1994 trip to the region.

Poland's ambitions in the West prevented it from standing too close to a Ukrainian state clearly unprepared for NATO or other Western institutions. A strategic partnership with Ukraine might well hamper its own chances of membership in these institutions. Moreover, as long as Ukraine delayed resolving the status of nuclear weapons on its territory, it remained a partner of questionable value to Poland's prospective Western partners. At least some Poles harbored the unspoken sentiment that Ukraine might not "make it" as an independent state. Given these doubts and constraints, Poland could quietly cajole the West toward a more favorable view of Ukraine, but it could hardly step into the spotlight as Ukraine's partner without diminishing its own standing.

Thus, after mid-1993, Ukrainian-Polish relations were of secondary importance for both countries. The old animosities stayed buried and the structures of consultation remained in place, but the momentum of the relationship came to a standstill. What was accomplished and preserved from the initial period was no small feat, but it hardly created the dynamic ties needed to bridge existing or future lines in the region. In a May 1995 speech before the Sejm—the Polish Parliament—former Foreign Minister Wladyslaw Bartoszewski gave Ukraine only a brief, warm mention, but offered no specific initiatives.[86] Some changes were stirring, however, that would give the relationship new life. Ukraine improved both its political and economic prospects, and Poland gained increasing but by no means airtight assurances on eventual NATO membership. Ukraine also took a cautious but forthcoming stand on NATO expansion and deepened its own ties with the Alliance.

In 1995, increasing worries about the direction of Russian policy once more shifted Ukrainian-Polish ties to center stage in both capitals. During the summer of 1995, senior officials from both sides met to consider ways of rejuvenating the existing structures of consultation. Poland played a key role in pressing for

---

[86] *FBIS Daily Report: Eastern Europe*, 25 May 1995. On getting Poland's eastern policy back on track, see Kazimierz Dziewanowski, "Grozby i szanse ze Wschodu," *Rzeczpospolita*, 26 May 1995.

Ukraine's full membership in the Central European Initiative in October 1995. Polish and Ukrainian defense ministers upgraded their defense ties, looking toward some forms of bilateral cooperation with NATO's Partnership for Peace program. Some momentum returned to bilateral ties—a momentum that President Kwasniewski continued with meetings between Polish and Ukrainian prime ministers as well as foreign and defense ministers in 1996, in preparation for the June Polish-Ukrainian summit in Warsaw. The summit itself was the culmination of a process that returned the bilateral relationship to a prominent place. Sustaining this momentum, however, will necessitate Ukrainian economic reforms that make Ukrainian-Polish economic cooperation more feasible. It will also require a NATO expansion process that meets Ukrainian (and Russian) concerns to preserve low levels of forces and a non-nuclear Central Europe.

A more cautious view of what is possible with Kiev remains widespread in policy-making circles in Warsaw. It was expressed quite clearly in September 1995 by then Polish Foreign Minister Wladyslaw Bartoszewski, who sought to ward off charges that the lag in Polish-Ukrainian relations was the fault of Warsaw: "I do not think the degree of readiness and political will is the same in Poland and Ukraine . . . [W]e can bring Ukraine closer to the structures of European security only to such an extent as they themselves want."[87] Bartoszewski and other skeptics in Poland would be right, of course, if Polish interest in Ukraine were charitable, but in fact Polish security is intimately bound up with the survival of a stable and independent Ukraine. Moreover, Poland's position in the West is greatly affected by whether or not it has stable neighbors. Yet there are many in Poland who would regard the security issue resolved the moment Poland entered NATO.

The prospect of NATO expansion has had serious distorting effects on policy in Poland and the other "Visegrad" states.[88] Polish officials have all along understood the importance of an independent and stable Ukraine for long-term Polish security,

---

[87] Interview with then Polish Foreign Minister Wladyslaw Bartoszewski, "Nasza polityka jest stabilna," *Tygodnik Powszechny*, 37 (10 Sept. 1995), pp. 1, 5.

[88] The "Visegrad" label—often used to refer to the Czech Republic, Hungary, Poland, and Slovakia—derives from the name of the Hungarian town where these countries formed an association in Feb. 1991 (when the Czech Republic and Slovakia were still Czechoslovakia).

yet this has not distracted them from focusing primarily on the politics of NATO. This orientation has encouraged senior officials in Central Europe to make statements—on foreign forces and nuclear weapons, for example—less as a matter of military strategy than as a signal to NATO of their desire to be full and loyal members. These statements have had predictably destabilizing consequences in the East.

It is obviously in Poland's interest to "build bridges" and sustain regional diversity, particularly through a strong relationship with Kiev. Traditionally, Poland has wrestled with two competing orientations: one focused on the West, the other on the East. Yet Polish *Ostpolitik* has taken a back seat in the march toward NATO. It is often argued that, like Germany, Poland must be firmly anchored in the West to conduct a confident and effective *Ostpolitik*. But Poland is not the divided Germany of the Cold War; Russia holds no Polish territory or ethnic Poles hostage as the Soviet Union held East Germany. Long-term Polish orientation toward the West is not in doubt. Today, Left and Right, however much they differ on policy prescriptions, display their common roots "in Europe." Poland's lack of confidence in its ultimate acceptance by the West (which Poland shares with the other Visegrad states) prevents it from seeing a vibrant *Ostpolitik* as a key element of its foreign policy. It is also a failure of the West not to see Ukraine and the other countries beyond the proposed new front-line of NATO as absolutely crucial to the success of a renewed and expanded Alliance. This failure to see that the axis of security has shifted east could well lie at the heart of NATO's future troubles.

UKRAINIAN-ROMANIAN RELATIONS

If Kiev's main challenge in its relations with Poland is building stronger ties, its central challenge with Romania is preventing a further deterioration in bilateral relations. Although Ukrainian-Romanian history records nothing like the tensions and tragedies of Ukrainian-Polish history, the two are divided over an unfinished friendship treaty. Three key issues dominate the bilateral agenda. Romania wants Ukraine to join it in a denunciation of the 1939 Nazi-Soviet Pact. It also wants clarification of the status of Serpent Island, located in the Black Sea near the mouth of the Danube. Ukraine, in turn, wants both sides to embrace long-standing principles of territorial recognition and bilateral relations codified by the 1975 Helsinki Final Act and subsequent Organization for Security and Cooperation in Europe (OSCE) agreements.

These issues are complicated in their own right; they potentially raise difficult questions about the status of the current Romanian-Ukrainian border. But their resolution is further complicated for both countries by their potential impact on even more important negotiations with a key neighbor. For Romania, that neighbor is Hungary; for Ukraine, it is Russia. There are nationalists in both Romania and Ukraine willing to promote a one-sided view of history, but these forces are outside the government and by no means a dominating force in the political life of either regime.

It is no surprise that the course of the negotiations has been rough, given the circumstances surrounding the talks between Kiev and Bucharest. After making little progress at negotiating sessions in autumn 1995, Ukraine recalled its ambassador to Bucharest for consultations in October. Although senior Romanian officials deny having any territorial claims on Ukraine, they insisted during negotiations on the importance of delineating territorial waters in a way that clarifies the status of Serpent Island. Talks resumed in November, with little progress. In December 1995, then Foreign Minister Teodor Melescanu stated that Romania's differences with Kiev over Serpent Island might well be taken to the International Court of Justice.[89] At a March 29, 1996 meeting between Ukrainian and Romanian prime ministers in Izmail, Ukraine, the two sides signed commercial and trade agreements, but made no progress on the core issues of the friendship treaty. Now that Hungary and Romania have concluded their bilateral treaty and a new Romanian president has been elected (in November 1996), a breakthrough is possible. Romania in fact has powerful incentives to reach agreement with Ukraine before the July 1997 NATO summit. Romania wants membership in NATO, and it cannot hope for admission while territorial issues with a neighbor are outstanding. The three issues and their possible connections to Romanian-Hungarian and Ukrainian-Russian negotiations are examined below.

---

[89] *OMRI Daily Digest*, 7 Dec. 1995.

On the Nazi-Soviet Pact issue, it is noteworthy that the legitimacy of Ukraine's current borders with Romania rests on precisely this treaty, in which Hitler gave Stalin the go-ahead to seize Northern Bukovyna and Southern Bessarabia. The Soviets issued Romania an ultimatum in June 1940 that led to Romania's ceding the regions to the USSR. These Soviet gains were confirmed in postwar treaties, and the two territories became part of the Ukrainian SSR and thus of present-day Ukraine. However, condemning the pre-war maneuverings of the two great powers at the expense of smaller and weaker neighbors is not simply a matter of squaring the historical record; it also potentially raises awkward questions about the legitimacy of current borders. Ukrainians understand that these regions were Romanian before 1940, but they became Romanian only in 1918, when they were seized from a weak imperial Russia. Ukraine's political leaders have little interest in Romania's settlement of historical scores. Just such grumbling about historical injustice fuels Russian opinion about the status of Crimea. Ukraine's primary concern is to ensure that its current borders are recognized. It certainly does not want to call into question its borders in the west for fear of undermining those in the east. A small minority in Ukraine even fear that this maneuver will encourage what they see as long-term Romanian designs on Moldova and Ukrainian territories as part of a "greater Romania."

Serpent Island, located east of the mouth of the Danube River, is a special subset of these territorial issues. It was awarded to Romania in 1878 in order to put a check on Russian ambitions to control the mouth of the Danube and its commerce. The Paris Peace Treaty of 1947 and a subsequent Soviet-Romanian agreement in a 1948 protocol made plain that Serpent Island, because it was east of the mouth of the Danube, was Soviet territory. Rumors of possible oil deposits in the Black Sea have complicated this question. Romania believes that the restriction of its claim on territorial waters as a result of these postwar treaties places it at a disadvantage in claiming a share of any potential energy development.[90]

---

[90] For a compelling explanation of Ukraine's strategic interests in Serpent Island, see Evenimentul Zilei, 22 Jan. 1996, p. 3 (translated in *FBIS Daily Report: East Europe*, 1 Feb. 1996).

Romania's resistance to embracing OSCE principles on borders and other matters almost certainly is linked to the still delicate negotiations under way with Hungary on a state treaty. In April 1996, the two sides reported progress in their talks, but the key issues remain minority rights for Hungarians in Transylvania and a bilateral commission to oversee the treaty's implementation. Romanian concessions to Ukraine on OSCE principles would support the basic Hungarian position on minority rights. It remains to be seen whether Romania is absolutely opposed to OSCE language and fears the potential use to which such language could be put, or whether it simply wants to reserve its concession on the issue for the more important negotiation.

Taken together, these unresolved issues could create serious and enduring tensions between Kiev and Bucharest, particularly if they weaken the legitimacy of Ukraine's current borders. Fortunately, there are inherent checks on both sides. Romania's main foreign-policy objectives are focused on Europe, particularly on the immediate goal of gaining membership in NATO. The Romanian military is looking ahead toward a future of professionalism and ties with the West—not one of reviving nationalist traditions and eastward expansion. Romania cannot hope to win membership or even favorable relations with European institutions while pursuing a policy of territorial revanchism. Ukraine, for its part, has its hands full with Russia; it wants to prevent any agreement with Romania from weakening its position in talks with Moscow.

In a Europe where many questions still linger about the legitimacy of borders and where violence plagues nearby Moldova and the former Yugoslavia, Romanian-Ukrainian negotiations should not remain a matter of indifference. Although conflict seems an unlikely result, the issues now accounting for tension between Bucharest and Kiev in the past have been the ingredients of many bloody and preventable wars.

MOLDOVA

The internal conflict in Moldova between its central government and the breakaway Trans-Dniester region has already erupted into a full-fledged civil war and drawn in Russia. It has the potential to draw in other outside powers, particularly Romania. After a desultory experiment with a four-power negotiation (involving Moldova, Romania, Ukraine, and Russia) to end the fighting in 1992, Russia assumed the role of arbiter, both through its forces deployed in the region and through its diplomatic intervention. The root of the problem is the largely ethnic Russian Trans-Dniester enclave in what was the Moldovan SSR. In the late Soviet period, as (Romanian-speaking) ethnic Moldovans asserted their rights—particularly through the election of a large number of members of the Moldovan Popular Front to the national parliament in 1990—ethnic Russians in the Trans-Dniester launched a campaign to protect themselves from "Romanization." In September 1990, the ethnic Russians of the Trans-Dniester declared the region's independence. In fall 1991, when Moldova became independent, the Trans-Dniestrians began a campaign to drive ethnic Moldovans out of the region. This ethnic tension was further complicated by the presence of the Soviet, and subsequently Russian, 14th Army. In Soviet times, the 14th Army was little more than a low-readiness, reserve structure—barely the size of a full-strength division.[91] In the current political and military context, however, it represents by far the greatest concentration of organized military force in Moldova.

Heavy fighting between Moldovan forces and the Trans-Dniestrians broke out in March 1992. In May, the 14th Army's commander reported to Moscow that he had lost control of his forces; in late June 1992, General Aleksandr Lebed (who briefly in 1996 served as head of Russia's Security Council) was appointed to the post. After the quadripartite diplomatic process failed to negotiate a ceasefire, Russia and Moldova negotiated their own and deployed a peacekeeping force in August. This force—which consists of six Russian, three Moldovan, and two Trans-Dniestrian battalions—has maintained a shaky peace since 1992, but there has been little progress on the basic political issues.

In August 1994, the Russian and Moldovan presidents reached agreement on the gradual withdrawal of the 14th Army over a period of three years, although the agreement also linked

---

[91] IISS's *Military Balance 1996-1997* (p. 115) estimates the troop strength of the unit at 6,400, with 120 main battle tanks.

the withdrawal to simultaneous progress on Trans-Dniester's legal status. The eventual withdrawal of this force remains an open question. General Lebed was relieved of his command in mid-1995. Little progress has been made between Moldovan and Trans-Dniestrian officials. Although Moldova has consistently offered the region sweeping autonomy, the Trans-Dniestrian leadership wants nothing short of independence (or integration with Russia). In October 1995, the Trans-Dniestrians adopted a "fundamental law" to serve as the constitution for the breakaway republic.

From Ukraine's perspective, Moldova poses several risks to regional security. Secessionist factions could once more turn to violence, which might spill over into Ukraine. The Trans-Dniester also poses a political problem—not only an ethnic and cultural one—for Moldova. The secessionist leadership doubtless regards Ukrainian independence with as little respect as it does Moldovan statehood. This leadership wants to see Russia—and a traditional, great-power Russia at that—maintain its presence in the region. The forces of the breakaway region by themselves present no real menace to Kiev, but the conflict they encourage weakens the Moldovan state and encourages outside intervention. The internal struggle has already altered Moldova's relationship to the CIS, with Moldova moving from its initial coolness toward the Commonwealth to reluctant participation. It has also given Russia a special role in Moldovan affairs. Should Moldova experience a crisis at the center, Romania also has an interest in the fate of the Romanian-speaking majority of this country. Moldova could well spark intervention from these two outside powers that also have interests and ambitions in Ukraine proper.

The withdrawal of the 14th Army, if it occurs, also poses potential dangers. The Moldovan government would like to see the entire 14th Army depart but—under current conditions within the Russian military—it is difficult to imagine a scenario in which the entire army and its equipment leave the region. The headquarters, commanding officers, and active personnel might leave, but there would be intense local pressure and the active collusion of some within the 14th Army itself to leave equipment in the hands of the separatists. Large amounts of equipment would probably be "diverted" to the Trans-Dniestrians before the withdrawal, leaving the already overmatched Moldovan army in a hopeless situation.

Ukraine, left out of the 1992 ceasefire agreement, has recently and cautiously begun to play a more active role in Moldova. It has strengthened its ties to the Moldovan government, signing both a military cooperation agreement (December 27, 1995) and a protocol on trade cooperation (January 10, 1996). The military agreement builds on a 1993 agreement, but Ukraine can offer only modest help to the under-equipped and under-trained Moldovan forces. Moreover, Ukraine knows that it cannot become an active sponsor of the Moldovan military without creating tension with Russia and Romania.[92] Ukraine has also re-engaged in the diplomatic process. In January 1996, at the CIS summit conference in Moscow, President Kuchma joined Moldovan President Mircea Snegur and President Yeltsin in signing a statement recognizing the Trans-Dniester region as a constituent part of Moldova.[93] Ukraine would like to see other international participants in the process; some Western European involvement would help shore up the Moldovan state and limit the possibility of either Russian or Romanian interference in Moldovan affairs. But such outside involvement, even by European states and organizations closest to the problem, seems unlikely.

Ukraine potentially has a positive role to play, as an honest broker, both in the diplomatic negotiations and on any eventual settlement that will almost assuredly include outside peacekeeping forces. Ukrainian participation in both elements of the process is also in Russia's long-term interest, for it would signal Kiev's first important step away from a policy of keeping out of conflicts within the former USSR. However, Ukrainian participation, particularly in the peacekeeping phase, is unlikely—even impossible—if the operation is carried out solely within the framework of the CIS. At present, Russia sees only the advantages of unilateralism, or at best a CIS-structure through which it plays the dominant role. For Russia, there are advantages in supporting a genuinely multilateral peacekeeping structure, provided that it retains a central role in the operation. These

---

[92] *OMRI Daily Digest*, 11 Nov. 1995, 28 Dec. 1995, and 11 Jan. 1996.
[93] *OMRI Daily Digest*, 23 Jan. 1996.

advantages include obtaining Ukrainian participation and support, as well as international backing, for an operation that has enjoyed neither. Such an operation comes at the price of Russia's current ability to run it however it likes. The Moldova problem is the most likely case in which Russia might be able to gain Ukrainian participation, but to do so, Russia would have to change its own way of thinking about the management of problems in the former Soviet Union.

NATO EXPANSION AND WESTERN INSTITUTIONS

One of the most important aspects of the new Central and Eastern Europe, aside from the return of the nation state, is the region's openness to the outside world. Central European intellectuals speak of a "return to Europe," although the states of the region have unequal prospects and face varying obstacles in undertaking such a "return." The region's return to the West is matched by the West's return to the region, which amounts to much more than the expansion of the NATO alliance, although that has attracted most of the attention and creates the greatest strategic dilemmas. The West's "return" includes entrepreneurs, investors, communications, and services, as well as new political, cultural, and even security ties. Over time, it will also include the expansion of the European Union to Poland, the Czech Republic, Hungary, and eventually perhaps Romania and one or more of the Baltic states.

In some very important respects, the solid foundations for this transformation of international relations in Central and Eastern Europe have been laid by the series of arms control and security agreements of the 1980s—agreements to eliminate intermediate-range nuclear forces, to lower drastically the levels of conventional forces, to establish confidence-building measures to enhance transparency and predictability, and to take tactical nuclear weapons off of the battlefield and off ships at sea. Within the region as a whole, there is a tension between the expansion of the "Western space," understood as its manner of doing business, and key Western institutions that bestow particular security or economic benefits. It should be a key preoccupation of those managing the expansion of the institutions to ensure the softest possible landing for the region as a whole.

In the near term, however, the most important security question is NATO enlargement. The imminence of NATO expansion in July 1997 into at least part of the region is already an important factor in defining the security "architecture" of the region as a whole. The success or failure of this endeavor—understood not simply as whether the Alliance gets new members, but rather whether the whole of Europe and NATO itself is more stable and secure as a result—will have lasting security ramifications. There will be reactions and adjustments regardless of the outcome. The purpose here is not to replay what is by now a rather tired debate about the pros and cons of this expansion, but to focus attention on the role that expansion has had and will have in shaping the region's security arrangements.

NATO expansion is creating a new dividing line. Because of the old dividing line in Europe, such talk is heresy for NATO officials and supporters of expansion, but the line is already emerging. The distinction between countries fully within and those just outside the NATO security structure is a potentially serious one. Poland will be a full member of the West by virtue of NATO expansion, but Ukraine, Belarus, and the Baltic states will not. The line will be important, not only for security reasons, but because it will address internal challenges to state-building—a point made on behalf of NATO expansion to Poland, the Czech Republic, and Hungary by its supporters.[94] This line should not be either a new Berlin Wall or the sole and defining security feature of the region—but it is there and should be acknowledged.

The line is based on the distinction between explicit and binding commitments offered NATO's prospective members and less binding assurances and good wishes that will remain the diplomatic daily fare for states like Ukraine. However, the role of less binding assurances, political commitments, and negotiated rules of the road should be of *greater*, not lesser, importance in the new Europe—unless it is the goal to extend NATO or a NATO-inspired collective security structure to every state in Europe. Moreover, it was precisely assurances, political commitments, and material assistance that bore such fruit for U.S. and

---

[94] Ronald D. Asmus, Richard L. Kugler, and F. Stephen Larrabee, "Building a New NATO," *Foreign Affairs*, 72: 4 (Sept./Oct. 1993), pp. 28-40.

Western diplomacy in Ukraine—preeminently on the nuclear issue, but subsequently across an array of complicated political, economic, and security issues. It is vital in the coming years to preserve the entire array of diplomatic tools to address the emerging Eastern and Central European security environment. It would do great damage to this environment if all the states of the region came to see the goal of their security policy as "NATO membership or nothing."

As the July 1997 NATO summit draws nearer, more attention is being paid to the problem of Alliance relations with those states that will be left outside the first wave of NATO enlargement. As a state that is not seeking Alliance membership and strongly opposes any enlargement at all, Russia is receiving the lion's share of attention from NATO and key NATO countries like the United States. A whole package of measures is under negotiation that is designed to give Russia a special mechanism for consultations with NATO on key security issues. Other related security measures, including new nuclear talks and further adaptation of the Treaty on Conventional Forces in Europe (CFE), are also being discussed. Negotiations with Ukraine on an agreement that would define a "special relationship" with NATO began only in late March 1997. Proponents of enlargement point to the Partnership for Peace (PFP), membership in the Council of Europe, and the multilateral, NATO-led peace-keeping operations in Bosnia as the very real start of such ties. For Ukraine and its neighbors who are likely to be left outside the new forward area of the Alliance, these measures are welcome, but hardly a solution to looming internal and external challenges. For Russia and the Russian military, only the Bosnian operation points toward the prospect of real and substantial military cooperation at a level that reflects Russia's experience and capabilities. As to possible European security mechanisms parallel to NATO, the real work lies ahead—with the model of the "contact group" on Bosnia offering the greatest promise.

Kiev's approach to NATO expansion is one filled with both fears and hopes. Ukraine's greatest fear is that the parallel track and other possible compensatory measures of any kind will seem less robust, or will be more difficult to develop in the atmosphere likely to mark the region after NATO expands. In the aftermath of expansion, the Alliance and its new members will have their own work of consolidation to do. Russia will undoubtedly for some time react negatively to the decision, and it is likely to take compensatory steps that directly affect Ukraine. NATO and Russia will dominate the resulting security environment, by their response and counter-response, even if these steps do not assume the military dimensions currently threatened in some Russian press reports. This cycle will be profoundly difficult for Ukraine and will directly threaten its current "breathing space" at a time when Ukraine's stability and survival are not yet clearly recognized in the West, particularly in Western Europe, to be a matter of great importance.

Ukrainian officials understand the value of NATO and its role in European security. They support NATO as a counterweight to Russian power. As such, it helps to preserve Ukraine's "breathing space" and permits it to consolidate its independence. Over the past four years, senior Ukrainian officials also have seen the value of anchoring Poland in the West, believing such a move would project stability beyond Poland. But these same officials are also preoccupied with managing the risk of expansion—by seeking both to expand Ukraine's own ties with the Alliance and to ensure that NATO takes steps to support a "soft landing" for the other states of the region outside the Alliance.[95] Some senior Ukrainian officials have begun to talk openly of the long-term possibility of Ukraine's membership in NATO. There is near unanimity that, at the very least, the door to NATO—and to other key European institutions—should be kept open.

Ukraine has never opposed NATO expansion. It has adopted a nuanced view of the process that begins with a clear acknowledgment that "each state has the right to decide itself on participation in any international organization or bloc."[96] Ukraine's interest in non-interference by outside states in basic security decisions is obvious. It has also gone further, supporting Poland's desire for membership in NATO, which President Kuchma described as "the only real guarantor of security on the continent."[97]

However, senior Ukrainian officials have warned against a "hasty expansion" that could leave Ukraine a "buffer" between the

---

[95] The author's interviews with senior officials in the ministries of defense and foreign affairs and with presidential advisors in 1995 and 1996.

[96] See statement by President Kuchma, reported in *ITAR-TASS*, 4 Oct. 1995.

[97] *Zycie Warszawy*, June 24, 1995, pp. 1, 6.

CIS and NATO.[98] President Kuchma has spoken of the need to take "considerable time" with the process of expansion. "I also think," he stated, "such a decision cannot be taken without taking into consideration Russia's views. It is a historical reality."[99] In the run-up to his June 1996 visit to Warsaw, Kuchma said: "[Y]ou cannot build a security system in Europe without Russia. Cooperation with Russia is currently the largest challenge for Europe and the world."[100] Many Ukrainians fear Russia's reaction to NATO expansion. A senior Ukrainian Foreign Ministry official underscored Ukrainian anxieties: "We have to begin thinking he said, in terms of what is good for Ukraine—to think in terms of our national interest . . . What does Ukraine get from this expansion?" He went on to detail his fears of renewed Russian pressure, a likely shift in the region's security geography owing to accelerated Russian-Belarusian integration, and the strong potential (in his view) for increasing neglect of Ukraine by Poland.[101]

Ukraine has also added its voice to those warning against militarizing the NATO expansion debate. In September 1995, former Polish Minister of Defense Zbigniew Okonski stated that Poland was prepared to support, as a member of NATO, the stationing of foreign forces and nuclear weapons on Polish soil.[102] In October—in a series of leaks that some Russian defense analysts believe were authorized by Russian Defense Minister Pavel Grachev himself—"unnamed military sources" sketched possible Russian conventional and nuclear counter-measures to NATO expansion.[103] Ukrainian Foreign Minister Udovenko offered a note of caution and warning. He criticized public and private Central European statements indicating a willingness to accept nuclear-weapons deployments and underscored that such deployments would seriously complicate the situation in Eastern Europe and threaten relations with Russia.[104] A similar plea for "playing down the military factor" was made by Ukrainian Prime

---

[98] Foreign Minister Udovenko's comments reported by *ITAR-TASS*, 14 Apr. 1995; and *Mlada Fronta Dnes*, 9 Oct. 1995, p. 9.

[99] Kuchma's interview on *Radio Ukraine World Service*, 4 Oct. 1995 (translated in *FBIS Daily Report: Central Eurasia*, 5 Oct. 1995); and *ITAR-TASS*, 4 Oct. 1995.

[100] *Polityka*, June 15, 1996, p.15.

[101] Author's interview, September 1995.

[102] *PAP News Wire*, 27 Sept. 1995.

[103] See, for example, articles in *Komsomol'skaya pravda*, Oct. 6, 1995; *Nezavisimaya gazeta*, 7 Oct. 1995; and *Segodnya*, 20 Oct. 1995.

[104] *OMRI Daily Digest*, 11 Oct. 1995.

Minister Marchuk during his October 1995 visit to Poland.[105] It has been a constant theme of Ukrainian senior officials ever since. In April 1996, President Kuchma put forward a plan at the Moscow Nuclear Summit for the creation of a Central European nuclear-weapons-free zone as a way to ensure that NATO expansion does not radically alter existing military realities.

As for Ukraine's own relationship with NATO, a senior foreign ministry official defined it on the eve of Udovenko's September 1995 trip to Brussels as "everything short of Article V"—that is, everything short of an explicit security guarantee.[106] This is precisely what the Ukrainian delegation laid out to NATO during that trip.[107] Former Prime Minister Marchuk and other senior officials have also called upon Russia to cooperate with NATO, or at least "not confront" it.[108] In addition, also in September 1996, Kiev transferred First Deputy Foreign Minister Tarasyuk to Brussels. This shift was inspired by power struggles within the Kuchma administration—not by a profound concern about managing Kiev's relationship with NATO and the European Union—but Tarasyuk's presence in Brussels has added skill, energy, and momentum to Ukraine's representation to these two key institutions. In March 1997, Foreign Minister Udovenko traveled to Brussels to begin negotiations on a NATO-Ukrainian "special partnership" document that would deepen and formalize Ukraine's relationship with NATO.

Ukraine's interest in NATO cooperation in fact began well before September 1995. In 1993, Ukraine enthusiastically welcomed NATO's Partnership for Peace program, recognizing that such a program was ideally suited for a country that was neither in line for membership nor demanding a special status that would differentiate it from the other countries in Europe. Ukraine was the first CIS country to seek participation in the program, and senior officials of the ministries of defense and foreign affairs worked hard to prepare an acceptable work plan. All along, however, the great constraint for Ukraine has been money. How far Ukraine gets in implementing a more active relationship with NATO will depend on its finding the budgetary

---

[105] *Rzeczpospolita*, 9 Oct. 1995, p. 8.
[106] Author's interview, September 1995.
[107] See *ITAR-TASS*, 11 Oct. 1995.
[108] *Rzeczpospolita*, 9 Oct. 1995, p. 8.

resources for such a relationship—and on the Western alliance and its members recognizing the importance of this new relationship and lending a helping hand.

Ukraine has made it clear that, while it is urging NATO to take account of Russia's views, interests, and historic role in the region, it does not share Russia's view of NATO expansion as a threat and will not participate in any strategy of counter-measures or new military blocs. In a newspaper interview in October 1995, President Kuchma rejected the notion that a new CIS military bloc is needed:

> The problem of creating new military blocs, including the CIS, is for me a problem of determining the functions of those blocs. While old military blocs often exist under their own momentum, in creating new ones you must always have a clear answer to the following questions: Why do you need to create them? Against whom do you want to create them? . . . And whom does Ukraine confront today? As of today, I do not see any global threat [or] challenge of aggression that would require the creation of a CIS military bloc. Naturally, there exist local tension spots in various regions of the Commonwealth, but neutralizing local threats requires local agreements.[109]

Thus the mainsprings of Ukraine's approach to NATO are, not surprisingly, the hope for a real partnership with the Alliance (perhaps even membership), balanced against serious concerns for the preservation of regional equilibrium—particularly the concern that NATO expansion will leave Ukraine exposed to renewed Russian pressure for political, economic, and security integration. Senior Ukrainian officials worry that, with the nuclear weapons finally removed, the West may no longer care about Ukrainian security. Others believe Ukraine's future is in the West, but that to reach this future, Ukraine must transform itself internally and avoid falling victim to Russian coercion in the interim.

NATO expansion places Ukraine's "breathing space" at some risk. It complicates regional security at a time when Ukraine is least able to manage such complications. Both Western

---

[109] *Zerkalo Nedeli*, 14-20 Oct. 1995, pp. 1-2.

advocates of NATO expansion and Russian advocates of integration divide the region between a "core" and an outer zone, with the core receiving full security ties. For the West, the core zone, though still undefined, includes Poland, the Czech Republic, and Hungary. For Russia, the core is the CIS. Both sides have notions of additional political and security measures for countries outside the core. The West began the Partnership for Peace program, open to all non-members and designed to increase practical interaction and cooperation with the Alliance. It is also debating other measures, such as special treaty ties. Russia has regularly proposed joint NATO–Russian (or NATO–CIS) security guarantees for the countries between the two security blocs. The interplay of NATO expansion and integration in the former USSR could be laying a foundation for security measures and countermeasures, and thus the return of a militarily significant rift in the region based on different security orientations.

The emerging new divide in Europe coincides with others—particularly the lines between those who have and those who have not significantly gained from market and political reforms, and between those with a strong state tradition and those still searching for stable institutional arrangements and the people to maintain them. Ultimately, all of these divisions have to be acknowledged as a first step toward bridging them. Pretending there are no consequences to NATO expansion for Ukraine—or that robust compensatory policies to limit negative consequences already are in place—is a recipe for disaster.

RUSSIAN-BELARUSIAN INTEGRATION

The leaders of both Russia and Belarus have long favored various forms of economic, political, and military integration, and in April 1996 they capped a series of agreements on integration by signing a treaty creating a "Community of Sovereign States."[110] For the states of the region and the West, the issue is

---

[110] The treaty text, "Treaty on the Formation of the Community," was published in *Rossiyskaya Gazeta*, 28 Oct. 1996, p. 9 (reprinted in *FBIS Daily Report: Central Eurasia*, 28 Oct. 1996). A summary of the Treaty's main points was provided in *Interfax*, 1 Apr. 1996. The statements of Presidents Yeltsin and Lukashenko at the signing ceremony—on both what the Treaty will accomplish and why it is in the interests of the Russian and Belarusian people—were published in translation by *FBIS Daily Report: Central Eurasia*, 2 Apr. 1996.

not so much whether Belarus disappears as a sovereign state—
for even the most sweeping forms of integration are unlikely to
return Belarus to the formal status of province—but rather
whether Belarus retains real control over its security policy on
key questions of the deployment and control of military forces
on its territory. For Ukraine, Poland, and other states of the
region, this is a problem of real strategic significance. A change
in the status of Belarus would shift the regional balance of power.
If Poland becomes a member of NATO, Belarus will increasingly become a matter of Alliance interest as well.

The roots of independence are much weaker in Belarus
than in Ukraine, and the desire to recreate linkages of one kind
or another with Russia is correspondingly stronger.[111] The orientation toward Russia is clear among both the leadership and
the people of Belarus.[112] Indeed, Belarus exemplifies the most
intensive integrationist trends within the former USSR; a series
of economic, military, and political agreements designed to
effect closer ties already is in place.

Belarus and Russia have been seeking economic integration since the agreement on a "new kind of ruble zone" in
September 1993, followed shortly thereafter by an agreement on
monetary union. In September 1994, Russian Prime Minister
Viktor Chernomyrdin stressed that monetary union was not
automatic but required Belarusian economic reform and privatization. In May 1995, a Russian-Belarusian customs union was
announced—yet another in a series of agreements suggesting
impressive momentum toward integration. But the history of
attempts at full economic integration has largely been one of
strong statements and agreements that regularly unravel as the
two sides face the pricetag of economic integration. For Russia in

---

[111] For a comparison of Belarus and Ukraine on the issue of national identity
and foreign policy, see Stephen J. Burant, "Foreign Policy and National Identity: A
Comparison of Ukraine and Belarus," *Europe-Asia Studies*, 47: 7 (1995), pp. 1125-
1144. An alternative view has been offered by George Sanford, "Belarus on the Road
to Nationhood," *Survival*, 38: 1 (Spring 1996), pp. 131-153.

[112] Polls conducted for USIA March 3-20, 1995 found a high degree of popular support for: the CIS (75 percent expressed confidence in the organization), monetary union with Russia (66 percent favor it), deeper political integration with Russia
(50 percent—though only 2 percent wanted Belarus to become part of the Russian
Federation). "Belarusians are Little Concerned about Foreign Threats" and
"Belarusians Like the U.S. but Prefer Closer Relations with Russia," *Opinion Analysis*
(United States Information Agency), 10 May 1995 and 15 Aug. 1995, respectively.

particular, the cost of a 1:1 exchange for Belarusian currency is enormous and has put the brakes on real integration.

In Russia, during the election season of the first half of 1996, almost no one spoke out *against* steps toward integration. In a November 1995 resolution, the Duma had called for accelerating the pace of Russian-Belarusian integration, and President Yeltsin embraced integration in general and Belarus in particular as a theme to strengthen his position in the presidential elections. His conclusion of two integration agreements in spring 1996 was loudly proclaimed a sign of Russia's renewed leadership and proof that strong integrative tendencies are truly on the rise in the former USSR. The treaties also served as Yeltsin's response to even more integration-minded Communist and nationalist politicians who led the March 1996 effort in the Duma to repeal the 1991 agreement ending the Soviet Union. Yeltsin again proposed accelerating the process of integration in January 1997. However, fiscal and material burdens remain as before, and they clearly shape the way integration is being presented and implemented. Yet the political forces in favor of integration remain strong in both countries.

Belarus has also moved steadily toward greater military integration with Russia. It modified its early embrace of neutrality by adhering to the Tashkent Treaty on Collective Security in 1993, although with reservations designed to keep its forces out of peacekeeping and other military deployments around the CIS. Belarusian diplomats have argued that adherence to the Tashkent Treaty is compatible with neutrality.[113] Russian-Belarusian military cooperation began in July 1992 with a series of agreements that settled basic questions on the status and support of strategic nuclear forces that remained in Belarus. These agreements were ratified by the parliaments of both nations in the first half of 1993.[114] A March 1994 military agreement

---

[113] Ural Latypov, "Neutrality as a Factor in Belorussian Security Policy," *Occasional Paper from the Conflict Studies Research Centre* (Royal Military Academy Sandhurst, February 1994). Latypov served in the Belarusian Foreign Ministry and helped to develop Belarus's policy of neutrality. The paper stresses the restrictions placed on Belarusian adherence to the Tashkent Treaty and the consistency between that commitment and neutrality.

[114] For a discussion of these 1992 agreements and an excellent overview of the Belarusian armed forces and the problems they face, see Richard Woff, *The Armed Forces of the Former Soviet Union* (Hampshire, England: Carmichael and Sweet, 1995), Vol. 2, Part 2, pp. E1-E31.

embraced a more expansive set of questions, including long-term access to Belarusian military infrastructure and joint border protection.[115] Technical agreements followed soon thereafter, permitting long-term Russian leasing of a naval communications site and an early-warning radar facility.[116]

Belarus signed the CIS Treaty on border protection between CIS and non–CIS states in July 1995. This treaty defines borders as "sections of the state borders of participants in the Commonwealth of Independent States with states that are not members."[117] In December 1995, Russia and Belarus agreed on further military cooperation, particularly measures to strengthen ties between the military-industrial enterprises of the two states, to expand joint use of Belarusian military infrastructure (especially in air defense), and to coordinate regional planning efforts. Even though the withdrawal of Russian strategic forces is scheduled to be completed by 1997, and no new Russian forces have been deployed, this pattern of close military cooperation has raised questions in light of President Aleksandr Lukashenko's warning that if NATO expands eastward, "we will have to redeploy in Belarus the nuclear weapons that were withdrawn from it."[118]

Many assume that the world will not be very different with Belarus tightly integrated with Russia. After all, Belarus has been slow in its pursuit of reforms, and its population does not seem all that interested in independence. President Lukashenko makes flattering comments about Hitler and regrets Belarus's agreement to dismantle all of the strategic nuclear missiles on its territory and send them back to Russia.[119] But at present the burden of Lukashenko falls on the unfortunate people of Belarus, not on the developing regional security system as a whole.

That system is marked by a profound reduction in nuclear and conventional military forces that benefits all of the states of

---

[115] *ITAR-TASS*, 11 Mar. 1994.

[116] *Krasnaya zvezda*, 24 May 1994, p. 3.

[117] The Treaty was published in *Rossiiskaya gazeta*, 7 July 1995, p. 4. The text of a parallel bilateral undertaking is contained in the May 1995 Treaty on Friendship (*Rossiiskaya gazeta*, 5 May 1995, p. 10).

[118] *Financial Times*, 19 Jan. 1996.

[119] For Lukashenko's comments on Hitler, see *Izvestiya*, 28 Nov. 1995. His statement on strategic missiles in Belarus was reported by *UPI*, 12 Jan. 1996.

the region. Both the states of the region and outside powers should encourage the legitimate activity of creating national armies down paths that reinforce, not undermine, this trend. Similarly, the building of security ties with outside powers, such as Belarus's relationship with Russia, should also respect that trend. There are few regional states with the resources to create a military in the near-term that could reverse this trend, though existing decisions on doctrine, exercises, weapons procurement, and redeployment of forces will have an impact.

At the center of the Belarus problem are the military consequences of the country's relations with Russia. Some of the steps to deepen Belarusian-Russian military ties have been labeled "counter-measures" to NATO expansion, although Russian interest in close military cooperation with Belarus predates any serious prospects for NATO expansion. NATO expansion does add legitimacy to such cooperation and to the possibility of counter-measures—if not in Western eyes, certainly in those of Russian political and military leaders. A reversal of the trend toward reduction in forces would have destabilizing consequences for Ukraine, the Baltic states, and the states of Central Europe.

Belarus's orientation toward Russia is already a regional factor. Many analysts consider Belarus today an appendage of Russia. But Belarus is still a country, and its military subordination to Russia has not yet assumed a definite character, particularly with regard to deployments of Russian forces and equipment. There is a world of difference between an anemic but independent state and a junior partner, or even pawn, of Russia. If Russian-Belarusian military integration occurs, a new "line of contact"—one of much greater potential military significance than the border between Poland and the isolated Russian outpost of Kaliningrad—will be created between NATO and Russia. Political tension along the new line will put additional pressures on Ukraine and the Baltic states to define their status and orientation.

Russian-Belarusian integration creates the prospect that any reconstitution of Russian power would have an immediate impact on Central Europe (and thus potentially on the new front-line states of NATO) because of the possibilities it would open up for the forward deployment of Russian forces.

Belarusian-Russian military integration would make a Russian response to NATO expansion significant for the Western Alliance; it would greatly increase the stress on NATO's new front line, and thus on regional stability as a whole. The new forward edge of NATO would not be a powerful and viable (albeit divided) country, as the Federal Republic of Germany was, but a much weaker Poland. It would be vulnerable to pressures on its eastern borders. Poland and the other Visegrad states do not have the resources to cope with potential refugee, corruption, narcotics, or economic disruptions spreading from their neighbors. Poland would also find it hard to respond on its own to new military deployments in Belarus. It would clearly turn to the NATO Alliance for help. Although any new military confrontation is unlikely to be as formidable as the old line of contact (it would take a decade or longer for Russia to re-gather even a semblance of the old Soviet force structure in East Germany), the new front line of the Alliance will be much more fragile, and could easily come under severe strain.

Belarusian integration with Russia would significantly complicate Ukrainian security policy; it would remove any doubt about Belarus's role in future Ukrainian-Russian frictions. While Russian forces returning to Belarus would obviously make use of existing infrastructure (which all points west), there would clearly be a temptation to build in flexibility for a Ukrainian contingency. Moreover, deployment in Belarus would create a new and serious planning factor for the Ukrainian military; it would add 900 km of border to worry about to a defense plan already overextended by the length and shape of its border with Russia.[120]

Successful integration with Belarus would serve for Russia as the model for integration elsewhere in the former USSR. After success in Belarus, looser integrative structures would appear to Russian observers less as alternative models than as failures. In the short run, success in Belarus could inspire a more ambitious Russian policy toward Ukraine, although the evident differences between the two countries would certainly reveal the

---

[120] Barry Posen, "Kontseptsiya Oborony Dlya Ukrainy" ["A Defense Concept for Ukraine"], *Ukraina: Problemy Bezopasnosti*, ed. Irina Kobrinskaya and Sherman Garnett (Moscow: Carnegie Endowment for International Peace, 1996)—also in *Safeguarding Ukraine's Security: Dilemmas and Options*, ed. Youri Matseiko and Steven E. Miller, forthcoming, (MIT Press).

limits of the Belarusian model. In the long run, the Belarusian model of deep integration has little attraction for states like Ukraine. Russia is likely to find that each success in Minsk presages another failure in Kiev.

This section would not be complete without at least an acknowledgment of the potential of a quite different problem arising in Belarus. At the end of 1996, profound tensions emerged between President Lukashenko and both the political opposition and members of the ruling elite. Lukashenko's drive to consolidate one-man rule and to accelerate the pace of integration with Russia, as well as his failure to address Belarus's basic economic problems, elicited street demonstrations and political opposition. The country's current stagnation and Lukashenko's unreliability have helped forces within Russia opposed to integration—or simply to the high cost of integration—to once again slow down steps toward integration. It is quite possible that the coming months could see a worsening of the Belarus economy, serious conflicts among the ruling elite, and even the appearance of social unrest. Such instability in Belarus would present all of its neighbors—Ukraine, Russia, Poland, the Baltic states, and the West in general—with a genuinely complex problem on which little advanced thinking or preparation is evident.

CONCLUSION

A new security environment is in the making in Eastern and Central Europe. Some of its main features are by no means new, but others are quite unprecedented, particularly the rise of and interaction among the new and restored states. It would be a great mistake to see what is happening in the region as a pause before the return of imperial history. The relations and divisions among the states are already a crucial factor in the region.

The main strategic challenge for the West is to fashion a set of policies that respond both to the region as a whole and to a hierarchy of interests within it. Problems of NATO expansion, the secure command and control of former Soviet nuclear weapons and materials, and the future of Russia will continue to represent first-order security interests for the West. However, these interests cannot be protected by policies that concentrate solely on Brussels or Moscow. The tension between U.S. policy toward Russia and NATO expansion has been obvious for some time. The states between Russia and NATO have a key role to play in determining the success or failure of both NATO expansion and continued stable relations with Russia. Changes in the region place constraints on Russian power and give the new and restored states unprecedented and growing influence. Many of these states and their problems may represent secondary or derivative security interests for the West, but Western interests that are today universally acknowledged to be of supreme importance—namely the NATO Alliance and the development of the European Community—will increasingly be hostage to the successes and failures of this new region and even of some of its individual new states.

CHAPTER 5

UKRAINE AND THE WEST: LESSONS OF NUCLEAR DISARMAMENT

The last Soviet warhead left Ukraine in mid-1996. Many factors, including Ukraine's own domestic politics, contributed to this successful outcome. What separates the nuclear issue from others, however, is the role played by the United States and other Western countries. U.S. engagement made a significant difference. Without it, the most likely outcome would have been not Ukraine's seizure of the weapons— such a move would have been too destabilizing internally—but a long stalemate in Russian-Ukrainian talks that would have brought the nuclear systems increasingly under *de facto* Ukrainian control. Even if other factors in Ukraine and Russia could be counted upon to prevent the nuclear issue from escalating to a nuclear confrontation, a delay in the momentum on Ukrainian disarmament could well have cast a pall over successful efforts in 1995 to extend the Nuclear Non-Proliferation Treaty (NPT) indefinitely. A delay would have added greatly to uncertainty in the region and would have further constrained Ukraine's internal search for consensus and reform, as well as the prospect of external support for both.

Indeed, there was no better way to develop a more positive approach to Ukraine and Ukrainian independence than that ultimately selected on the nuclear question. Many critics of earlier handling of the issue, including this author, believe that the final and successful U.S. policy approach—mixing incentives for expanded political relations and economic reform with continued firmness on nuclear disarmament—should have been tried from the very beginning, not after nearly two years of misunderstanding and mutual recriminations. The nuclear issue could not have been indefinitely postponed while U.S.–Ukrainian political and economic relations developed normally.

The nuclear question unfolded in three distinct phases, the

first of which can be described as a stage of declarations and romanticism on the Ukrainian side and great anxiety on the part of the West. It lasted until mid-1992. The intentions of the Ukrainian side during the first period are well represented by the Rada's 1990 resolution affirming the country's status as a neutral and non-nuclear power. In Kiev, there were great expectations, both moral and material, of global support. Western leaders, on the other hand, feared the impending collapse of the USSR; they trusted Soviet President Gorbachev more than the promises of a still uncertain legislative body. In private, they feared—and exaggerated—what President Bush expressed publicly during his August 1991 visit to Kiev on the very eve of Ukrainian independence: the dangers of "suicidal nationalism." Formal U.S. recognition of Ukrainian independence, when it came in December 1991, was conditioned on fulfillment of Ukraine's pledge to become a non-nuclear state.

The second phase began with the signing of the Lisbon Protocol in spring 1992 and ended with the U.S.–Ukrainian–Russian Agreement in January 1994. For the West, the Lisbon Protocol settled the status of nuclear weapons on the territories of Ukraine, Belarus, and Kazakhstan. The Soviet successor states became part of the Strategic Arms Reduction Treaty (START) by committing to the early ratification of START I and accession to the Nuclear Non-Proliferation Treaty as non-nuclear weapon states "in the shortest possible time." Yet what appeared to the West to be the end was for Ukraine only the beginning. The Ukrainian leadership was coming face to face with the realities of statehood. Internally, economic hardship and regional tensions seemed to challenge the very notion of Ukraine's survival. The relationship with Russia was reaching its first real hurdles, with tensions surfacing in spring 1992 over possession of the Black Sea Fleet and other issues. The Ukrainian leadership was also slowly coming to understand the massive costs associated with fulfilling its nuclear commitments. Thus, for Ukraine, the hard part of negotiations began *after* the Lisbon Protocol. Needless to say, Ukraine's wavering, after signing the Lisbon Protocol, initially was viewed in the West as a lack of good faith. In fairness, there were other factors, particularly Ukraine's lack of experience in judging what it required and what it should get for its agreement to the Lisbon Protocol. The $150 million in aid linked to Ukrainian agreement was in fact hardly adequate for starting, let alone sustaining, the costs of dismantling and transfer of nuclear warheads and the safe elimination of the silos and delivery systems left behind. The nuclear issue was not of Ukraine's making, and its resolution was not of major concern to Ukraine alone. U.S. assistance was not only money well spent; it was vital to supporting a process of disarmament that accorded with vital national interests. This crucial middle phase lasted from mid-1992 until the conclusion of the Trilateral Agreement in January 1994.

The third phase was one of implementation of Ukraine's nuclear commitments and the broadening of U.S.–Ukrainian ties. It began with the Trilateral Agreement in January 1994 and came to an end in June 1996 with the removal of Ukraine's last nuclear weapons. During this phase, Ukraine formally acceded to the NPT as a non-nuclear-weapon state and received a set of security assurances from the NPT depository states. Though much still remains to be done to complete work on silos and delivery systems, the period after June 1996 can be genuinely characterized as a post-nuclear one, in which the shape of the relationship will be determined by a broad set of political, economic, and security—not nuclear—issues.

It was during the second phase that the United States confronted the bleakest options for dealing with Ukraine and decided upon a course that led to broadening political, economic, and security ties with Ukraine. How the United States arrived at that course is best understood by examining three key policy crossroads of the period: (1) the spring 1993 U.S. policy review; (2) the response to the Rada's conditional ratification of START I in November 1993; and (3) the conclusion of the Trilateral Agreement itself in January 1994.[121]

THE SPRING 1993 U.S. POLICY REVIEW

By late 1992, it was clear to Washington policy-makers that the Lisbon Protocol could not be implemented without U.S. engagement and involvement. The Bush administration attempt-

---

[121] The next three sections rely heavily on the author's article, "The Sources and Conduct of Ukrainian Nuclear Policy: November 1992 to January 1994," in *The Nuclear Challenge in Russia and the New States of Eurasia*, ed. George Quester (Armonk, NY: M.E. Sharpe, 1995).

ed to broaden its approaches to Ukraine at that time. There was a single, high-level Ukrainian visit to Washington, by Deputy Foreign Minister Tarasyuk, but a broad strategic dialogue with the Bush administration did not develop, given President Bush's defeat in November. The transition to a new administration and its early concentrated focus on supporting Russian reform left Ukraine on the back burner until the early spring of 1993.

The Ukrainian government, prodded by critics in the Rada and the desire to secure political and economic support from the West, moved away from its earlier stress upon "negative control" and dismantling within Ukraine in favor of the notion that nuclear disarmament in Ukraine should be linked to specific economic and security conditions. From at least fall 1992 on, the Ukrainians stated explicitly that getting from commitments in principle to the actual dismantling and withdrawal of nuclear warheads would require a real negotiation. At a November 1992 press conference, President Kravchuk said that Ukraine should have "appropriate compensation" for nuclear disarmament and, in addition, "certain guarantees" for its security. He repeated this message frequently in late 1992 and early 1993.

Nevertheless, Washington expected the Ukrainian Rada to address at least the ratification of START I in January 1993. Under the Lisbon Protocol, President Kravchuk had committed Ukraine to ratification of START I and accession to the Nuclear Non-Proliferation Treaty as a non-nuclear-weapon state in the shortest possible time, but January came and went. On February 10, 1993, the speaker of the Rada stated that START ratification was not a priority.[122] On February 18, the Rada formally postponed consideration altogether. In April, 162 deputies signed an open letter "on Ukraine's nuclear status." The letter underscored Ukraine's status as a successor to the USSR, including "as a nuclear power." It confirmed Ukraine's "right of ownership of the nuclear weapons on its territory" and emphasized the importance of compensation and of "state independence, national security, and territorial integrity."[123]

---

[122] *Ostankino Television*, 10 Feb. 1993 (translated in *FBIS Daily Report: Central Eurasia*, 11 Feb. 1993).

[123] The letter reads in part: "[E]ven prior to the ratification of START I, a whole complex of problems needs to be resolved. This applies in particular to the question of

The Russian side, recognizing the drift in Ukrainian domestic opinion, advocated redoubled efforts and diplomatic pressure to bring about Ukrainian compliance. Moscow press reports regularly warned of a possible safety issue as the Ukrainian side took over administrative control of nuclear and other military sites. The best example of the Russian approach occurred later in the year, at the September 1993 Russian-Ukrainian summit meeting in Massandra, Crimea.

At this meeting, Russian leaders exerted considerable pressure on President Kravchuk to agree to a comprehensive deal on the Black Sea Fleet, nuclear disarmament, and debt relief. The centerpiece of this Russian package was a swap of at least partial debt forgiveness for Ukraine's share of the Black Sea Fleet. But the Russians overplayed their hand. They misjudged their capacity to impose a comprehensive deal and Kravchuk's power to accept and enforce it. The results of the Massandra summit split the Ukrainian government so severely that any hope for the agreement quickly unraveled. Prime Minister Kuchma, one of those who favored the swap of the Ukrainian share of the Black Sea Fleet for debt relief, resigned in early September 1993. An open split developed between President Kravchuk and Defense Minister Morozov, who resigned in October 1993 because he favored Ukrainian insistence on complete Russian withdrawal from Crimea as the *sine qua non* of a deal on the Black Sea Fleet.

In the aftermath of the Massandra summit, the Russian side saw that Ukrainian weakness was not simply something to be exploited; it was also a danger to regional stability and to the Russian-Ukrainian relationship as a whole. With this increasing Russian concern about Ukrainian stability came a growing if reluctant appreciation that progress in nuclear talks required financial and other incentives that could only be provided by the United States in a trilateral framework. Massandra convinced

---

compensation for the nuclear materials that were taken out of the warheads of the tactical nuclear weapons that had been transferred from Ukraine to Russia in the spring of 1992, to the guarantees of destroying these weapons by Russia, and to the enormous financial expenditure on the reduction of the nuclear potential . . . At the same time it would be a mistake to agree to promises of insignificant monetary compensation in exchange for Ukraine's immediate nuclear disarmament. The question of nuclear disarmament, state independence, national security, and territorial integrity cannot become an object for bargaining or "monetary compensations." *FBIS Daily Report: Central Eurasia*, 30 Apr. 1993, p. 51.

the Ukrainian side, particularly President Kravchuk, that Ukraine's internal weakness was seriously affecting the stability of the government. Indeed, Kravchuk listed the Massandra summit as one of the two major problems he faced during 1993: "Russia then in Massandra saw how hard the strikes [summer 1993 miners' strikes] were hitting Ukraine and that it was brought to its knees by internal problems. On top of that there was external pressure, and people were taking advantage of our weakness."[124]

President Kravchuk understood that there would be no sustained financial aid or security ties without resolution of the nuclear question. A bilateral negotiation with Russia would result in pressure that Ukraine could not control. There is little doubt that Kravchuk's experience in Massandra—where he encountered intense Russian pressure and deep division within his own government on the Black Sea Fleet issue—played a key role in his decision to accelerate negotiations with the United States and to seek a trilateral framework for resolving the nuclear issue.

No such strong sense of a need for trilateral negotiations or for an expanded agenda was prevalent in the U.S. government. In fact, the prevailing U.S. mood was a mixture of anxiety over long-range Ukrainian nuclear intentions and anger about Ukraine's failure to fulfill its obligations. Although no formal linkage existed between nuclear disarmament and economic assistance, Washington could not sustain even modest assistance while Ukrainian nuclear intentions were uncertain.

In early 1993, the U.S. government began to review its Ukrainian policy. No one in the U.S. government questioned the basic nuclear elements of the policy, and no serious player—in fact, no player at all—advocated tolerance for a Ukrainian nuclear deterrent. The nuclear elements of the policy remained: to continue to press Ukraine to fulfill its obligations and to provide financial assistance for this purpose. Differences in views did emerge, however, over whether the key to Ukrainian compliance was to expand the U.S. policy of engagement or to tighten the screw still further. The review ended with a decision to engage Ukraine in a broad discussion of improved economic,

---

[124] *Izvestiya*, 31 Dec. 1993.

political, and security ties, implementation of which would be linked to the resolution of the nuclear issue. In May 1993, then U.S. Ambassador-at-Large Strobe Talbott visited Kiev to discuss a "turning of the page" in U.S.–Ukrainian relations. Discussions between Ukraine and the United States focused not only on outstanding nuclear matters but also on economic assistance, expanded military and defense ties, and a renewed political relationship between the United States and Ukraine. In essence, the U.S. side sought to sketch the kind of relationship that could arise once the nuclear problems were removed. This initial visit did not reverse months of mutual suspicion, but it did begin a process that brought senior levels of both governments together in an atmosphere of give-and-take on the full set of issues.

Ambassador Talbott's visit was quickly followed by Secretary of Defense Les Aspin's visit to Kiev in early June. Aspin came directly from a meeting with Russian Minister of Defense Grachev, in which the two sides discussed U.S. proposals for early dismantling of nuclear systems in Ukraine. These proposals included arrangements for international monitoring designed to meet Kiev's concerns about the dismantling, transfer, and final dispensation of the warheads. Ukrainian Minister of Defense Morozov visited Washington in July, promising cooperation on dismantlement. Regular diplomatic consultations and correspondence continued, including discussions on economic, political-military matters, and defense relations in October. By the time of Secretary Christopher's visit to Kiev in October 1993, the U.S.–Ukrainian dialogue had been restored. A genuine trilateral negotiating process had also emerged, bringing together Ambassador Talbott, Russian Deputy Foreign Minister Georgi Mamedov, and Ukrainian Deputy Foreign Minister Tarasyuk for regular discussions.

THE CONDITIONAL RATIFICATION OF START I

In November 1993, the Rada conditionally ratified START I. The resolution laid out a number of conditions and demands. Some appeared to define the conditions for a nuclear deal; others, particularly the unilateral amendment of the Lisbon Protocol, seemed to be trying to scuttle the trilateral talks.

Kravchuk and other senior officials quickly reassured the United States, Russia, and the world that the Rada's action was not the final word on the matter. It would be wrong, however, to see the Rada's action solely as an act of defiance. The links between the senior levels of the Kravchuk government and of the Rada ensured that, whatever the Rada as a whole had originally intended, the November ratification became a basis for the January 1994 Trilateral Agreement. Indeed, according to some of the key players, the resolution itself was drafted in the President's office and sent to the Rada, where it was approved with little modification.[125]

For the West, the resolution presented real problems. Neither the United States nor Russia could consider it a legally acceptable ratification of START I. The resolution declared that Ukraine was not bound by Article V of the Lisbon Protocol—which committed Ukraine to become a party to the NPT as a non-nuclear weapons state "in the shortest possible time." It reasserted Ukraine's claim to ownership of the weapons and set forth a series of conditions that would have to be met before its ratification would be legally binding on Ukraine.[126]

The dilemma in Washington was clear: Should this text be read as shutting the door or opening it? A case could be made that the Rada had finally gone too far, overturning the Lisbon Protocol and seeking the right to retain under START a significant portion of the nuclear warheads on Ukraine's territory. However, the text also contained specific conditions that could be read as a formal negotiating proposal on security assurances, compensation, and other key issues. In several places, the text made plain that these conditions were not final or gave the President of Ukraine latitude to negotiate further. Even in point six of the resolution, which claimed that Ukraine was bound by START to eliminate only a portion of the weapons on its territory, there was language stating that this formulation "did not preclude the possibility of the elimination of additional delivery vehicles and warheads according to procedures that may be determined by Ukraine." Points five and eleven explicitly asked the President of Ukraine to negotiate with other parties, and

---

[125] Author's interviews in Kiev, Sept. 1995.
[126] For the text of the resolution, see *Golos Ukrainy*, 20 Nov. 1993.

point twelve asked the President to approve a schedule and exercise control over the elimination of the nuclear systems to be dismantled. These points were important in Washington's assessment of the resolution.

Washington could never accept the Rada's explicit rejection of Article V of the Lisbon Protocol as a permanent statement of Ukraine's obligations, but it could explore the basis of an interim deal that would lead to a reconsideration of this statement. In essence, Washington acknowledged that START and the NPT had been temporarily de-linked, and that an interim agreement might be required for that linkage to be restored. It is clear from subsequent negotiations and the conclusion of the Trilateral Agreement that Washington in the end chose to interpret the Rada's action as at least something that could be overcome and perhaps an opening of the door. Eight weeks later, the Trilateral Agreement was signed, with the Rada rescinding its November resolution and ratifying START without conditions in February 1994.[127]

THE TRILATERAL AGREEMENT

By the end of 1993, the new U.S. policy toward Ukraine and continued bilateral and trilateral negotiations had put in place the basic foundation for agreement. In Ukraine, the growing sense of crisis, brought on by economic and political demands of striking miners in June and the Massandra summit in September, made the need to resolve the nuclear issue more pressing. Washington began to see in Ukraine's actions an opportunity to move forward. The announcement on December 20, 1993, that Ukraine would de-activate twenty SS-24s was considered in Washington a clear signal that President Kravchuk and his government were going to find a way to complete negotiations and deal with the Rada. Indeed, without some prior understanding with at least the senior leadership of the Rada, Kravchuk would not have risked taking such a step with regard to the SS-24s. Moscow was also interested in a deal that would preserve the basic framework of Massandra and begin the process of nuclear disarmament in Ukraine. The Russians

---

[127] The text of the resolution on START ratification was distributed by UNIAR, 3 Feb. 1994.

understood that the United States brought energy and financial resources to the arrangement and that U.S. presence ensured that progress on the nuclear question would not be reversed by some future bilateral issue, as had happened in the aftermath of Massandra. The Russians were also sure that, on the nuclear question, U.S. and Russian interests coincided. The Russian side trusted the U.S. side, even when tactical differences emerged, to advance the common agenda of achieving a non-nuclear Ukraine.

On January 14, 1994, Presidents Clinton, Kravchuk, and Yeltsin signed the Trilateral Agreement in Moscow. This agreement explicitly linked Ukraine's nuclear disarmament to its broader economic and security conditions, although opinion in Ukraine is divided over whether the agreement goes far enough. The significance of the Trilateral Agreement was that it provided a multilateral framework within which to address nuclear and other issues. It legitimized U.S. interest in issues that would ordinarily remain bilateral matters between Moscow and Kiev.

The nuclear portions of the agreement committed Ukraine to the "elimination of all nuclear weapons, including strategic offensive arms, located on its territory in accordance with the relevant agreements and during the seven year period as provided by the START I Treaty . . . "[128] Ukraine agreed in particular that "all nuclear warheads will be transferred . . . to Russia" and that "all SS-24s on the territory of Ukraine will be deactivated within 10 months by having their warheads removed." Within the same time period, "at least 200 nuclear warheads from RS-18 (SS-19) and RS-22 (SS-24) missiles will be transferred from Ukraine to Russia for dismantling." Ukraine was guaranteed compensation for the highly enriched uranium, beginning with 100 tons of low enriched uranium underwritten by a U.S. advance payment of $60 million. These provisions reaffirmed Ukraine's commitment to complete nuclear disarmament over the period of START implementation. President Kravchuk also agreed to maintain pressure on the Rada to accede to the NPT as a non-nuclear state, which it did in October 1994. The sides agreed on concrete interim steps for early de-activation of all SS-24s, a good-faith

---

[128] For the text of the Trilateral Agreement, see *RFE-RL Research Report*, 3:4 (28 Jan. 1994), pp. 14-15.

beginning on the transfer of warheads to Russia, and Russian compensation for Ukraine. Unlike previous agreements, the Trilateral Agreement provided performance standards against which Ukrainian (and Russian) behavior could be judged.

Three additional elements distinguished the Trilateral Agreement from previous Russian-Ukrainian agreements or even the Lisbon Protocol. First, both in principle and in practice, the Agreement established a truly trilateral framework in which to address future issues. U.S. involvement brought needed financial resources and technical expertise, of course, but also important experience in seeing agreements implemented. Previous Russian-Ukrainian negotiations had at best reached agreements in principle only to founder in the technical follow-up. The U.S. presence added balance to a situation that could easily be derailed if it remained bilateral.

Second, the Agreement provided for security assurances that were formally extended to Ukraine by the United States, Russia, and the United Kingdom once Ukraine acceded to the NPT as a non-nuclear-weapon state. These assurances fell far short of the kinds of guarantees that Ukrainian negotiators and parliamentary leaders regularly demanded. Yet they provided the strongest language on the recognition of existing borders to which Russia has ever agreed—since, as noted above, both the RSFSR–Ukrainian SSR Treaty and the Minsk accord on the establishment of the CIS referred to the recognition of territorial integrity only "within the framework of" the USSR or the CIS. These assurances, based on existing language in Conference on Security and Cooperation in Europe (CSCE) documents and the NPT, provided basic pledges that the powers would refrain from the threat or use of force against Ukraine, that they would not employ measures of economic coercion, and that they would not use nuclear weapons against Ukraine. These assurances were political, not legally binding. For Ukraine, they probably represented the best deal obtainable. Their real worth would be determined in the months ahead—as Ukraine tested their efficacy and particularly U.S. willingness to engage on issues outside nuclear disarmament.

Finally, the Agreement commited the United States to further technical and financial aid. President Clinton promised "to expand assistance" beyond the minimum of the $175 million already envisaged. A subsequent visit of economic experts from Ukraine to Washington in January 1994 laid the groundwork for an increase in dismantling assistance to $350 million. The Agreement also provided important momentum for the U.S.–Ukrainian economic relationship. President Kravchuk's visit to Washington in March 1994 led to an agreement to double economic assistance to $350 million. Ukraine has since moved to third place among the recipients of U.S. foreign aid.

The Trilateral Agreement was only the first step toward a final resolution of the nuclear question in Ukraine. Subsequent efforts to implement this Agreement, both on the political side (NPT accession, the formal exchange of security assurances) and on the technical side (the actual dismantling and transfer) have brought the sides to the end of the transfer process. This success undoubtedly was rooted in the spring 1993 shift in U.S. policy; while the United States continued to adhere to a strict insistence on Ukrainian nuclear disarmament, it began to engage Ukrainian concerns more broadly.

Success on the nuclear issue has inspired an expansion of U.S. political and financial support for Ukraine. But reward for past behavior should not indefinitely remain the justification of this approach. The question is: will the legacy of Ukrainian nuclear disarmament prove a help or a hindrance to the West's finding and sustaining a successful long-term policy toward Ukraine and the region as a whole?

CHAPTER 6

SHAPING A "POST-NUCLEAR" WESTERN POLICY

Ukraine's burden of establishing stability both internally and in its relations with its neighbors falls squarely on Ukriane's shoulders, but the West's engagement can play an important role in Ukraine's success. Western political and economic support is crucial to sustain the still weak forces of reform within Ukraine itself. Foreign aid and technical assistance, particularly from the IMF and the World Bank, are key factors in sustaining the transition to a reformed economy. Other forms of Western assistance also have been and continue to be important. It is likely that nuclear weapons would still be in Ukraine were it not for the U.S.–led trilateral negotiating process. The role played by the IMF clearly contributed to Russian-Ukrainian agreement on a debt rescheduling. In short, strategically focused outlays of Western political and economic resources have paid enormous dividends and could do so in the future.

RECENT TRENDS

In mid-1995, with the nuclear issue behind it, Ukraine began a series of policy initiatives aimed at expanding ties with the West. In September 1995, Foreign Minister Udovenko led a high-level delegation to NATO to begin to define a special relationship between Ukraine and the Alliance. In April 1996, addressing the Council of Europe Parliamentary Assembly in Strasbourg, President Kuchma said that Ukraine aims to become a full-fledged member of the European Union. In June, he reiterated his support for Polish membership in NATO. Ukraine has also worked to improve bilateral ties with key European states; the September 1996 visit of German Chancellor Helmut Kohl to Kiev yielded a range of agreements designed to broaden the base of German-Ukrainian relations. In September, the United

States and Ukraine agreed to establish a standing governmental commission to advance the bilateral agenda in foreign policy, military cooperation, economic reform, and trade and investment; in October, the two sides declared their relationship "a strategic partnership."

Ukraine's now considerable ties with the United States remain the bedrock support of Ukraine's turn to the West. These improved relations were slow to come—long stymied by the nuclear question and Washington's initial view that placing Russia first as a strategic priority necessarily meant placing Ukraine lower on the list. The resolution of the nuclear question opened the door to an expanded U.S. engagement with Ukraine, pursued for its own sake as well as to sustain the implementation of the nuclear accords. Ukraine is now the third largest recipient of U.S. foreign assistance. It has consistently received the attention of Secretary of State Warren Christopher and Secretary of Defense William Perry, who have made frequent visits to Kiev. In May 1995, President Clinton visited Kiev and was enthusiastically greeted by officials and the public alike. Senior Ukrainian officials count on continued U.S. support to help address a range of internal issues, particularly a sustainable energy policy, as well as to keep an eye on the status of unresolved issues with Russia.

Ukraine's interest in an expanded relationship with the West is quite clear. Even a West with heavy domestic economic commitments has the material resources and political influence to help Ukraine address its internal challenges, sustain the current "breathing space," and manage relations with Russia. But what are the West's interests in Ukraine? The United States recognizes the importance of Ukraine—as, increasingly, does Germany—but other countries in Western Europe lag far behind. This discrepancy has potentially serious consequences as further European energy and resources are directed toward the absorption of Poland and the other Visegrad states into NATO and the European Union. Yet none of the Western powers, including the United States and Germany, have based their approaches to Ukraine on a clear understanding of *long-term* strategic interests.

The ultimate handling of the nuclear issue provides impressive evidence that consistent and serious Western engagement can help to stabilize Ukraine, the Ukrainian-Russian relationship, and the region. However, the circumstances that led to this particular engagement are unique. The fate of the Soviet nuclear arsenal remains a matter of supreme strategic interest. No other issue of this unquestioned magnitude is on the Ukrainian-Russian relations horizon. Thus U.S. nuclear policy success in Ukraine is a mixed legacy: it demonstrates what can be accomplished by engagement with Ukraine and the region, but it also sets a standard that cannot be duplicated on non-nuclear issues.

In many respects, Western policy is now riding on the momentum created by nuclear disarmament and sustained by President Kuchma's economic reforms. But there is division in Washington and other Western capitals between those who see a new set of interests justifying an expanded policy toward Ukraine, and those who expect U.S. efforts to wind down now that the last warhead has been removed. The latter group does not see the necessity of sustained political, economic, and security ties with Ukraine. This division is unlikely to surface in the fair weather that U.S.–Ukrainian relations now enjoy, but it surely will re-emerge when ties with Ukraine demand hard political, economic, or security choices.

U.S. domestic priorities and resource constraints would seem to encourage a reduction in commitments abroad. Yet there is little doubt that the West would have to become involved directly in a major crisis of Ukrainian statehood or of Ukrainian-Russian relations, first and foremost because of geography. Ukraine is too close to a vulnerable Central Europe to assume that a crisis there could be contained. U.S. and Western interests in Ukrainian stability will only grow if Poland becomes a member of NATO. Furthermore, the most commonly heard alternative to Western engagement in a future crisis involving Ukraine—Russian intervention—makes little sense. Even if this were a desirable policy option, Russia is currently too weak to assume such a role. Russian attempts to intervene directly in Ukrainian politics would escalate a crisis, not control it. If the United States chooses to withdraw from Ukraine because it perceives its job to be done, it will face the paradox of not wanting to overextend itself when the costs are low but almost inevitably having to take part in a crisis when the costs are high.

Ukraine will continue to be a crucial factor in Russia's self-definition as a major power. The West has a stake in seeing Russia and Ukraine develop strong bilateral ties on a normal state-to-state foundation. It does not want to see, scattered on the edge of expanded Western security and economic communities, the preconditions for major inter-state conflict. It has an interest in the resolution of outstanding Ukrainian-Russian differences, the settlement of the Black Sea Fleet issue, and the emergence of a stable Crimea as an integral part of the Ukrainian state. "Getting the Ukrainian-Russian relationship right" is an essential part of the U.S. policy of supporting political and economic reform within Russia. Such internal progress in Russia depends upon a stable external environment and Russia's reconciliation with this new environment.

However, a policy for Ukraine cannot be reduced to a simple extension of the two major strands in Western policy to date: NATO expansion and Western policy toward Russia. Ukrainian membership in NATO is not in the offing. Nor can Ukraine's problems and prospects be consigned to the Russian sphere. Ukraine's unique problems compel Western policy-makers to think about the countries between NATO and Russia. These countries hold the key to whether Western plans for NATO and for cooperation with Russia are compatible. The success or failure of the countries beyond the Alliance will determine how much NATO expansion will cost.

TOWARD A MORE REGIONAL APPROACH

The West as a whole must now define—and then sustain for the long term—new policy goals that will enhance security and internal cohesion for Ukraine and the region as a whole. Six important building blocks of such a policy are suggested below.

1. Define U.S. and Western interests in the region. The West must understand what is at stake in Ukraine, particularly in the event of its internal failure or external frictions with Russia. From this perspective, a whole host of issues not captured by—and potentially complicated by—NATO expansion or Russian policy demand attention, including CIS integration, regional conflicts, and the basic building-blocks of independence and prosperity for the states of this region. The implementation of a sophisticated *regional* policy requires understanding of events in places such as Kiev, Warsaw, and Minsk. Strained U.S. and Western resources and domestic preoccupations would seem to urge against a sophisticated, multilateral approach to the region. Yet it is precisely these resource constraints, together with the recent history of U.S. policy success with relatively small resources, that make small investments in the region attractive.

2. Preserve and expand the mechanisms for cooperation, leverage, and influence already in place. Existing mechanisms grew out of the nuclear period of relations, but their utility extends far beyond nuclear issues. In the long run, the trilateral negotiating framework is as important as the Trilateral Agreement itself. It is an additional security assurance given to Ukraine that—while it falls short of an absolute guarantee from the United States— promises U.S. engagement (and that of the West in general) in a broad range of questions crucial to Ukraine and Ukrainian-Russian relations. This structure is unlikely to survive the end of the nuclear disarmament process without continued U.S. investment of diplomatic time and energy as well as funds.

The need for this kind of investment is by no means self-evident in Washington, and it is actively resisted in Moscow. When the Ukrainian Ambassador to Washington paid his respects to the departing Russian Ambassador in early 1994, the Ukrainian Ambassador suggested that both men drink a toast to the recently concluded Trilateral Agreement as a model for resolving future issues. The Russian Ambassador responded that the trilateral approach was fine for nuclear issues, where U.S. and Russian interest coincided, but that such a mechanism was not in Russia's interest on other Russian-Ukrainian issues, where U.S. and Ukrainian interests are more likely to overlap.[129] Many Russian political leaders share this view.

It is also important to be candid about U.S. views. The current positive stance toward Ukraine is built upon past nuclear accomplishments and provides only an emerging and imperfect sense of what U.S. long-term interests are in the region. The durability of the positive relationship has not been tested by the kind of internal adversity or external challenge that would force

---

[129] Author's interviews, Sept. 1995.

the United States and other Western powers to define just how much sympathy and politically binding assurances are worth in a pinch. There are still senior U.S. policy-makers who would be surprised, upon re-reading the Trilateral Agreement, at how strongly the United States committed itself to pay attention to other, post-nuclear security issues in Ukraine.

Formal trilateralism, particularly at the senior levels, has almost disappeared since early 1994. The high-level group led by U.S. Deputy Secretary Talbott, Russian Deputy Foreign Minister Mamedov, and Ukrainian Deputy Foreign Minister Tarasyuk has been disbanded. Foreign ministers and heads of state have not met trilaterally since early 1994—not even at the December 1994 Budapest meeting under OSCE auspices, where the last step in the nuclear disarmament process was carried out with the formal offering of security assurances by Russia, the United States, and the other NPT depositary, the United Kingdom. In January 1996, the defense ministers of Ukraine and Russia and the U.S. Secretary of Defense did meet in Ukraine, where they pressed the detonation device to destroy an SS-19 missile silo. They met again in June to celebrate the completion of warhead transfers, but little effort was made to turn the agenda toward the Black Sea Fleet or other "post-nuclear" questions.[130]

The drift away from trilateralism by definition removes many Ukrainian-Russian issues of importance from the immediate and easy reach of U.S. and Western policy-makers. If Ukrainian-Russian relations were to experience moments of tension or even crisis, U.S. influence would be easier to exert if mechanisms of consultation did not have to be created anew in a difficult context. Particularly as NATO expansion decisions are made, the re-establishment of a strategic dialogue at the deputy foreign minister level is crucial. Trilateral discussions should also be held regularly at the defense minister level. A trilateral perspective needs to permeate the bilateral meetings of the parties, particularly the rare but important meetings between heads of state. Perhaps the U.S.–Russian agenda is already overburdened

---

[130] The Defense Department has offered technical advice on the Black Sea Fleet issue, including dispatching experts on basing agreements, compensation, and other issues to talk to both sides. The Ukrainians were eager; the Russians, not so.

with problems, but it is important that Ukraine and Russia be aware of Western interest in the normalization of their relations and the settlement of outstanding questions between them.

3. Focus on Western European and Japanese economic involvement. The United States must encourage its allies to deepen ties with Ukraine. With the exception of Germany, Western Europe has barely "discovered" Ukraine. The European Union has a partnership and cooperation agreement with Kiev, but European officials are still skeptical of Kiev's long-term prospects and orientation, and Europe's view of Ukraine is dominated by the specter of nuclear disaster at Chernobyl. Ukraine's slow economic reform remains a sticking point with Europe: the overabundance of Ukrainian steel, chemicals, and agricultural products makes long-term EU–Ukrainian economic cooperation difficult. Following the early (failed) pattern of U.S. nuclear policy, the Western European countries have individually—and collectively through the European Union—taken a one-sided view of Ukraine's problems and importance. Japan has provided—reluctantly—only nuclear-related aid. Both Western Europe and Japan must now see how closely prospects for Eurasian security, and particularly the European Union's hopes for continued prosperity in Western and Central Europe, are tied to the future of Ukraine and of Ukrainian-Russian relations and events in Eastern Europe.

4. Preserve the basic support for military stability already present in the region. The low levels of conventional forces, the reduced strategic nuclear presence, and the absence of battlefield deployments of tactical nuclear weapons create favorable military conditions in the region—certainly the most favorable in several generations. These conditions are the result of the swift political changes that have taken place since the 1980s, reinforced by a set of arms control treaties that only partially regulate these forces. NATO expansion, deepening CIS military integration, and unilateral defense decisions by states of the region could reverse the momentum toward a stable military balance at lower force levels. Decisions in all three of these key policy areas must be informed by a common interest in preserving and stabilizing the current military situation in the region.

5. Determine a clear policy on CIS integration. It is not enough for U.S. policy to state that integration in the former

131

USSR should be voluntary. Nor is it a constructive response to look upon all integration as merely the resurrection of Russian imperialism. Some of the weakest states of the former Soviet Union are likely to see their future survival very closely tied to cooperation with Russia. The United States should adopt a policy on CIS integration close to that of current Ukrainian policy. Integration must not undermine state sovereignty or have adverse security consequences for the region as a whole. It must be open to the outside world. The United States has a stake in ensuring, for example, that Russian-Belarusian security cooperation does not develop in a way that reverses the trend toward lower levels of military force in Eastern and Central Europe. The Tashkent Treaty at this point poses little threat to the West. Now is the time for the West to make clear its view that future security decisions within the Tashkent Treaty or other CIS security structures must be compatible with regional and all-European security. Integration among the now independent republics of the former Soviet Union should be open to the broader integrative trends sweeping the globe and compatible with the broader decentralizing and regionalizing trends as well. The goal should be a regime that encourages rather than stifles individual enterprise on the part of the new states as well as regional ties among them.

6. Strengthen U.S.–Ukrainian relations. Ukraine presents the United States with the special challenge of more clearly defining the U.S. role in the new Eastern and Central Europe. For the United States, the question remains how best to fashion a Ukrainian policy that protects the United States' overarching security interests—in nuclear issues, in the moderation and transformation of Russian power, and in regional stability. This study has argued that these interests can best be protected by strengthened engagement with Ukraine and the region. Such engagement should not cede Ukraine to some mythical Russian geopolitical space or force the United States to play the role of a constant counterbalance to Russia. Neither role is consistent with U.S. interests or capabilities.

A policy of engagement in Ukraine requires a definition of U.S. interests not chained to Cold War thinking about spheres of interest. It requires that the United States work toward an outcome in which Russian power is moderated both by its own internal transformation and by the success of its neighbors, which are no longer sources of instability in their own right or pawns of any great power. Russia has had little experience with such neighbors. Its own policies since the eighteenth century are a principal reason for this lack of experience. It is not impossible, but it is unlikely, that Russia and its neighbors will be able to work out this kind of relationship on their own. There clearly is a role for the United States and its allies in encouraging the emergence of a genuinely *regional* system, but it requires that the United States understand the power it has to shape a new order in the region—in particular its interests in and influence over the stability of Ukraine and of Ukrainian-Russian relations.

With the passing of the Cold War and the emergence of crises in regions unknown to most Americans, the temptation is strong to narrow U.S. policy focus and limit U.S. commitments. The experience of the past three years' work on the nuclear issue, on Russian reform, and on the stability of Ukraine strongly counters this temptation. U.S. and Western power and influence will remain an instrument of consequence to the future stability of Central and Eastern Europe and Eurasia. Learning how to use that instrument in a new security environment is the challenge facing the post–Cold War generation of Western statesmen.

CONCLUSION:
KEYSTONE IN THE ARCH

In 1993, a group of analysts, journalists, and diplomats from the former Soviet Union visited the Pentagon. On that occasion, I gave a short presentation on U.S. policy toward the region and then asked if there were any questions. A Belarusian journalist asked whether, given the problems of political transition, economic collapse, and regional conflict, we would not all have been better off if the Soviet Union had remained intact. I responded that the world would perhaps be less uncertain, but we would certainly not be better off. I doubted whether, even with the best efforts of leaders like Mikhail Gorbachev and Eduard Shevardnadze, so gargantuan a country with such a political tradition could truly have completed the *perestroika* reforms. Moreover, it had been increasingly apparent that the option of preserving the USSR would more likely have depended on a re-tightening of the system than on a further loosening. Finally, I argued that the creation of these new medium-size and small states gave Eurasia a chance to organize the lives of individuals and of societies and states as a whole around systems more compatible with individual liberty and economic prosperity. There was no guarantee it would turn out all right, of course, but there was no turning back. You could either fear the future, or embrace it.

That future is upon us. The appearance of Ukraine and other new states on the territory of the former Soviet Union represents a profound and irreversible strategic shift. It is one to which the neighbors of these new states—especially Russia and the West as a whole—must adjust. For a time it seemed, at least to some, that such an adjustment would be unnecessary. Ukraine would not consolidate its independence or stabilize its economy. But Kiev has made substantial strides toward both goals. It is not necessary to be sympathetic to Ukrainian national aspirations to come to terms with this fact. One has only to be a realist. The problems of Ukrainian stability and of the stability of Ukraine's relations with Russia are part of the European security agenda—whether we want them to be so or not.

Ukraine's size, location, and the need to continue the work of internal reforms and consolidate its statehood make it an awkward fit in the new Europe. It no longer "belongs" to Russia, yet it is unable to make a credible near-term claim on Europe's core institutions. Its internal political, economic, and ethnic divisions proved less dangerous to the state than was at first feared, but they have complicated Ukraine's pursuit of political and economic transformation. Russia is not Ukraine's natural enemy, but the two sides have not found a way to place their bilateral ties on a normal, state-to-state footing. Ukraine's ties with Poland, Romania, Belarus, and other states in the region will help determine whether the various regional divisions that do and will exist—divisions of economic and political stability or security orientation—will be mitigated by strong bridges. As a state facing enormous challenges, Ukraine has been quicker than the West itself to understand the role that the West could play in Ukraine. Western policy has relied on a few critical issues to give it definition: nuclear disarmament, Chernobyl, economic reform. A sustainable policy, however—one that rests upon a clear view of the region as a whole and Ukraine's crucial place within it—is still wanting.

The preceding chapters have sought to provide an understanding of Ukraine and of Central and Eastern Europe under these new strategic conditions. Such an understanding is the first step toward a sustainable policy. This book also has suggested several key elements of such a policy. These recommendations can and should be debated. There is plenty of room for disagreement—particularly given existing resource constraints and a range of policy priorities well beyond this region, or even beyond Europe. But any discussion of priorities requires that we understand Ukraine, Russia, and the region in light of new trends, prospects, and constraints. An enlightened Western policy requires an appreciation of the stakes.

This book has argued that the long-term Western stakes in Ukraine are high. The West may well be free to forego the costs and troubles of near-term engagement, but it will not be able to avoid the higher costs of long-term failure. Ukraine is the keystone in the new security arch that stretches from the Baltic Sea to the Black Sea. It cannot be isolated or walled off from Russia or the West. Its stability and prosperity make regional stability and prosperity more likely. Instability or tension in its relations with Russia make its own stability and prosperity impossible. Fortunately, there is no immediate crisis on the horizon. But this state of affairs is only partly the result of foresight and wise policy. No one who has closely observed the events in the former Soviet Union since the late 1980s should fail to see that good luck has played a large and generous role in events there. No one who understands human affairs should fail to see how easily this luck could change.

SUGGESTED READINGS

Author's Note: A number of books and articles not cited in the text influenced the author's understanding of Ukraine. They are listed below.

Dominique Arel, "Voting Behavior in the Ukrainian Parliament: The Language Factor," in *Parliaments in Transition*, ed. Thomas F. Remington (Boulder: Westview, 1994), pp. 125-158.

Dominique Arel and Andrew Wilson, "Ukraine under Kuchma: Back to 'Eurasia," *RFE-RL Research Report*, 3: 32 (19 Aug. 1994), pp. 1-12.

John A. Armstrong, *Ukrainian Nationalism* (Littleton, CO: Ukrainian Academic Press, 1980).

Ian Bremmer, "The Politics of Ethnicity: Russians in the New Ukraine," *Europe-Asia Studies*, 46: 2 (1994), pp. 261-283.

Douglas Clarke, "The Battle for the Black Sea Fleet," *RFE-RL Research Report*, 1:5 (31 Jan. 1992), pp. 53-57.

_____. "The Saga of the Black Sea Fleet, *RFE-RL Research Report*, 1: 4 (24 Jan. 1992), pp. 45-49.

John Jaworsky, *Ukraine: Stability and Instability*, McNair Paper No. 42 (Washington, DC: National Defense University, 1995).

Gennadiy Korzh, "Ostrov zmeinyy v obshchem kontekstye Ukraino-Rumynskikh otnosheniy," *Nezavisimost'*, 22 Dec. 1995.

Taras Kuzio, *Ukrainian Security Policy* (Washington, DC: The Center for Strategic and International Studies, 1995).

John W. R. Lepingwell, "Negotiations Over Nuclear Weapons: The Past as Prologue?," *RFE-RL Research Report*, 3: 4 (28 Jan. 1994), pp. 1-12.

_____, "The Trilateral Agreement on Nuclear Weapons," *RFE-RL Research Report*, 3: 4 (28 Jan. 1994).

_____. "Ukraine, Russia and the Control of Nuclear Weapons," 2: 8 (19 Feb. 1993), pp. 4-20; "Beyond START: Ukrainian-Russian Negotiations," *RFE-RL Research Report*, 2: 8 (19 Feb. 1993), pp. 46-58.

Jeremy Lester, "Russian Political Attitudes to Ukrainian Independence," *The Journal of Communist Studies and Transition Politics*, 10: 2 (June 1994), pp. 193-233.

Ustina Markus, "Black Sea Fleet Dispute Apparently Over," *Transition*, 1: 13 (28 July 1995), pp. 30-34.

_____. "The Ukrainian Navy and the Black Sea Fleet," *RFE-RL Research Report*, 3:18 (6 May 1994), pp. 32-40.

Juliusz Mieroszewski, "Imperialism: Theirs and Ours," *Between East and West. Writings from Kultura*, ed. Robert Kostrzewa (New York: Hill and Wang, 1990), 39-40.

N. N. Moklyak, G. N. Perepelitsa, and S. A. Farenik, *Fenomen voenno-politicheskogo konflikta v sovremennoy etnopoliticheskoy situatsii* (Kyiv: Institut natsional'nikh otnosheniy i politologii NAN Ukraïny, 1995).

Arkady Moshes, *Vnutripoliticheskoe razvitie i vneshnaya politika Ukrainy v 1991-1995 gg.*, Occasional Paper of the Institute of Europe No. 27 (Moscow: Russian Academy of Sciences, 1996).

Alexander J. Motyl, *Dilemmas of Independence: Ukraine After Totalitarianism* (New York: Council on Foreign Relations, 1993).

_____. "Will Ukraine Survive 1994?" *The Harriman Institute Forum*, 7:5 (Jan. 1994), pp. 3-6.

Bohdan Nahaylo, "The Shaping of Ukrainian Attitudes Toward Nuclear Arms," *RFE-RL Research Report* ,3: 4 (28 Jan. 1994), pp. 21-45.

V. S. Nebozhenko, *Sotsial'na napruzhenist' i konflikty v ukrains'komu suspil'stvi* (Kyiv: Abrys, 1994).

John S. Reshetar, *The Ukrainian Revolution, 1917-1920: A Study of Nationalism* (Princeton: Princeton University Press, 1952).

Ivan L. Rudnytsky, "Observations on the Problem of 'Historical' and 'Nonhistorical' Nations," *Modern Ukrainian History* (Edmonton, Alberta: Canadian Institute of Ukrainian Studies, 1987), pp. 37-48.

_____. "Polish-Ukrainian Relations: The Burden of History," *Poland and Ukraine Past and Present* (Edmonton, Alberta: Canadian Institute of Ukrainian Studies, 1980), pp. 3-31

David Saunders, "What Makes a Nation a Nation? Ukrainians since 1600," *Ethnic Studies*, 10 (1993), pp. 101-124.

Roman Solchanyk, "The Politics of State Building: Center-Periphery Relations in Post-Soviet Ukraine," *Europe-Asia Studies*, 46:1 (1994), pp. 47-68.

_____. "Russia, Ukraine and the Imperial Legacy," *Post-Soviet Affairs*, 9:4 (1993), pp. 337-365.

Orest Subtelny, *Ukraine: A History* (Toronto: University of Toronto, 1988).

Roman Szporluk, "After Empire: What?" *Daedalus*, 123: 2 (Summer 1994), pp. 21-39.

_____. "Reflections on Ukraine After 1994: the Dilemmas of Nationhood," *The Harriman Review*, 7:7-9 (Mar.-May 1994), pp. 1-10.

_____. "The Ukraine and Russia," *The Last Empire: Nationality and the Soviet Future*, ed. Robert Conquest (Stanford, CA: Hoover Institution Press, 1986), pp. 151-182.

_____. "Dilemmas of Russian Nationalism," *Problems of Communism* (July-Aug. 1989), pp. 15-35.

Mark von Hagen, "The Dilemmas of Ukrainian Independence and Statehood, 1917-1921," *The Harriman Institute Forum*, 7: 3 (Jan. 1994), pp. 7-11.

Andrew Wilson, "The Growing Challenge to Kyiv from Donbass," *RFE-RL Research Report*, 2:33 (20 Aug. 1993), pp. 8-13.

Andrew Wilson, "Ukraine as a Nationalizing State. Will the 'Russians' Rebel?", a paper prepared for the Conference on "Peoples, Nations, Identities: the Russian-Ukrainian Encounter," Columbia University, 21-23 September 1995.

ACKNOWLEDGMENTS

The writing of a book is a solitary act, but gathering the information, arguments, and perspectives for it is decidedly a social one. This book is no exception to the general experience; it owes its existence to the help and encouragement of a good number of people—many more than I shall be able to enumerate below.

My introduction to independent Ukraine came in the Office of the Secretary of Defense, where I worked for ten years. I was lucky enough to work on Ukrainian and Russian issues for Secretaries of Defense Cheney, Aspin, and Perry. I could have asked for no better preparation for this book than my period of government service. But this book would never have been written without the opportunities opened up for me when Morton Abramowitz in 1994 asked me to join the Carnegie Endowment for International Peace. From the very beginning, what has made the Endowment the best imaginable place to study the issues of the transition of the former Soviet Union has been my colleagues—both at the Carnegie headquarters in Washington and at the Endowment's public policy research center established in 1993 in Moscow.

I must also thank a number of people in Ukraine and Russia for their time and perspectives. In particular, I want to thank a group of senior Ukrainian officials who helped me see past Ukraine's troubles to its future. These include some of the best diplomats now working—Borys Tarasyuk, Anton Buteyko, Konstanyn Hryshchenko, Yury Shcherbak, and Ihor Kharchenko; former and current senior officials in the Ukrainian government, especially Volodymir Khorbulin and Yevhen Marchuk; and serving and retired military officers Konstantyn Morozov, Volodymir Petenko, Oleksandr Skipalskyy, Vadim Hrechanninov, Hrigoriy Perepelitsa, and Ihor Smeshko. I am also grateful to Slavko Pikhovshek, Ivanna Klympush and the staff at the Ukrainian Centre for Independent Political Research, Oleksey Haran, Dmytro Pavlyyuk, Ihor Markiv, Markian Belinsky, and Grigoriy Nemiria. In Russia, I had help from my colleagues at the Carnegie Moscow Center: first and foremost, from Irina Kobrinskaya, co-director of the seminar we jointly run on Russian Foreign Policy at the Carnegie Moscow Center, and from Vladimir Vershinin, my Moscow-based research assistant. I am also grateful to Arkady Moshes, Igor Torbakov, Yury Dubinin, Aleksandr Golts, Pavel Felgengauer, Aleksey Arbatov, Vyacheslav Nikonov, Aleksey Pushkov, Sergey Karaganov, Vitaliy Portnikov, and many other scholars, journalists, and Russian officials who have taken part in our Moscow and Kiev seminars. I also wish to express thanks to The Pew Charitable Trusts for providing the basic funding for my research and travel, as well as for the three seminars held in Ukraine, sponsored by the Carnegie Endowment jointly with the Centre for Independent Political Research in 1995.

A number of people read the manuscript and offered criticisms and suggestions for improvement, including: Stephen Burant, Thomas Carothers, Lynne Davidson, Orest Deychakiwsky, Nadia Diuk, Maria Drohobytsky, Paul Goble, Rose Gottemoeller, Robert Hutchins, Antoni Kaminski, Matthew Kaminski, Dick Kugler, Yuri Luik, Alexander Motyl, Richard Murphy, Ilya Prizel, Eugene Rumer, Stephen Sestanovich, Roman Solchanyk, Jack Sontag, Fred Starr, Roman Szporluk, and Anne Witkowsky. This book would have been a much poorer product without their help.

There would be no book at all without my research assistants, Anita Seth and Elizabeth Reisch. The Carnegie Library staff of Jennifer Little, Kathleen Daly, and Christopher Henley took months off the research of the book by locating material for me. Valeriana Kallab provided much appreciated editorial advice and saw the book through to publication. Maria Sherzad prepared the final manuscript for the printer, entering and reentering corrections and changes, always accurately and with dispatch. David Kramer and Melissa Eustace have endured all too much of my drafting and redrafting, but they have willingly responded each time with improvements to the text; they provide much of the essential glue that holds together both my work and the work of the Endowment's Russian and Eurasian Program as a whole.

I also wish to acknowledge the help and encouragement of my friends, Thomas Graham, Nadia Schadlow (the U.S. Defense Department's first Ukrainian Desk Officer and the person from whom I learned the most about Ukraine), and Andrew Weiss. Finally, I am grateful to my wife, Jill, and our children, Sara, Anna, and Patrick, who indulged my great desire to write this book and put up with my too frequent trips to Russia and Ukraine

144

ABOUT THE AUTHOR

Sherman W. Garnett is a Senior Associate at the Carnegie Endowment for International Peace, where he specializes in the foreign and security policies of Ukraine, Russia, and other newly independent states of the former Soviet Union. Before joining the Endowment in 1994, he served for nearly ten years in the Office of the Secretary of Defense, working on a wide range of arms control and security issues. During his government career, he served as the Secretary of Defense's Representative to the Conference on Security and Cooperation in Europe and the Negotiations on Conventional Armed Forces in Europe. In 1993, Dr. Garnett became the Deputy Assistant Secretary of Defense for Russia, Ukraine, and Eurasia. He received his Ph.D. in Russian literature from the University of Michigan in 1982.

THE CARNEGIE ENDOWMENT
FOR INTERNATIONAL PEACE

The Carnegie Endowment for International Peace was established in 1910 in Washington, D.C., with a gift from Andrew Carnegie. As a tax-exempt operating (not grant-making) foundation, the Endowment conducts programs of research, discussion, publication, and education in international affairs and U.S. foreign policy. The Endowment publishes the quarterly magazine, *Foreign Policy*.

Carnegie's senior associates—whose backgrounds include government, journalism, law, academia, and public affairs—bring to their work substantial first-hand experience in foreign policy. Through writing, public and media appearances, study groups, and conferences, Carnegie associates seek to invigorate and extend both expert and public discussion on a wide range of international issues, including worldwide migration, nuclear nonproliferation, regional conflicts, multilateralism, democracy-building, and the use of force. The Endowment also engages in and encourages projects designed to foster innovative contributions in international affairs.

In 1993, the Carnegie Endowment committed its resources to the establishment of a public policy research center in Moscow designed to promote intellectual collaboration among scholars and specialists in the United States, Russia, and other post-Soviet states. Together with the Endowment's associates in Washington, the center's staff of Russian and American specialists conducts programs on a broad range of major policy issues ranging from economic reform to civil-military relations. The Carnegie Moscow Center holds seminars, workshops, and study groups at which international participants from academia, government, journalism, the private sector, and nongovernmental institutions gather to exchange views. It also provides a forum for prominent international figures to present their views to informed Moscow audiences. Associates of the Center also host seminars in Kiev on an equally broad set of topics.

The Endowment normally does not take institutional positions on public policy issues. It supports its activities principally from its own resources, supplemented by nongovernmental, philanthropic grants.

**Carnegie Endowment
for International Peace**
2400 N Street, N.W.
Washington, D.C. 20037
Tel.: 202-862-7900
Fax: 202-862-2610

Carnegie Moscow Center
Mosenka Plaza
24/27 Sadovaya-Samotechnaya
103051 Moscow, Russia
Tel.: 7-095-258-5025
Fax: 7-095-258-5020

COMING IN JUNE 1997:

RUSSIA AFTER COMMUNISM

Edited by Anders Åslund and Martha Brill Olcott

Five years have passed since the collapse of the Soviet Union, and Russia has evolved a new political and economic system. This book offers an overall assessment of what has been accomplished, what has failed to date, and where Russia is heading. The study is a unique collaborative effort, with the major issues examined by pairs of leading Russian and American scholars in jointly written analyses.

Michael McFaul and Nikolai Petrov analyze the Russian elections since 1989 and assess voting behavior. Scott Bruckner and Lilia Shevtsova address the question of whether Russia has become a stable pluralist society. Martha Brill Olcott and Valery Tishkov focus on the nature of the Russian nation as well as regional relations. Russia has become a market economy, but what kind of capitalism is being formed? Anders Åslund and Mikhail Dmitriev examine the continuing challenge of economic reform.

Anders Åslund and Martha Brill Olcott are senior associates at the Carnegie Endowment for International Peace (Washington, D.C.), which since 1993 has operated a Moscow Center for public research now comprising eighteen Russian and American scholars. Stephen Sestanovich heads the Endowment's work on Russia and the other newly independent republics in both Washington and Moscow. Scott Bruckner directs the Endowment's Moscow Center. All of the other contributors but one are senior staff members of the Endowment. Nikolai Petrov is a research fellow at the Institute of Geography of the Russian Academy of Sciences and a consultant to the Moscow Center.

ISBN: 0-87003-151-1 (paper) $16.95

UNFINISHED PEACE

REPORT OF THE INTERNATIONAL COMMISSION ON THE BALKANS

"*Unfinished Peace,* remarkably well written for a product of group-think, has a moral force which lifts its prescriptions far above the level of the normal policy institute paperback."
—*The New York Review of Books*

"Superb report"—*Newsweek (international edition)*

Members of the Commission: Leo Tindemans, *Chairman;* Lloyd Cutler, Bronislaw Geremek, John Roper, Theo Sommer, Simone Veil, and David Anderson *(ex officio).* Jacques Rupnik served as the Commission's executive director.

The guns have fallen silent in the former Yugoslavia. But the Dayton truce has yet to become a lasting peace. Peace in the Balkans remains threatened not only by the possibility of a new war in Bosnia, but also by unresolved conflict in Kosovo and Macedonia.

The International Commission on the Balkans was established in July 1995 by the Aspen Institute Berlin and the Carnegie Endowment for International Peace to provide an independent perspective on the region's continuing problems and to propose a concerted Western approach to long-term stability.

Drawing on its extensive, high-level, and politically comprehensive discussions throughout the region, the Commission examines the causes of the recent Balkan conflicts and provides an independent assessment of the European, American, and U.N. responses to them. It calls for a wide range of stabilizing measures—including proposals for the treatment of minorities, the promotion of democracy, and Balkan cooperation. To be effective, the Commission warns, such efforts must be reinforced by NATO's continuing and coherent military engagement.

ISBN: 0-87003-118-X (paper) $14.95

To order (by charge card), please call Carnegie's distributor, Brookings Institution Press, toll-free at 1-800-275-1447, or call 202-797-6258. Fax: 202-797-6004. When ordering, please refer to code TKEY.